# SYMBOLS SIGNS AND SONGS

# OTHER IDAHO BOOKS BY RICK JUST

*Idaho Snapshots*
*Keeping Private Idaho (a novel)*
*100 Years — Idaho and Its Parks*
*Images of America, Idaho's State Parks*
*A Kid's Guide to Boise*
*Fearless — Farris Lind the Man Behind the Skunk*

Copyright © 2020

**CEDAR CREEK PRESS, LLC**

ISBSN 978-0-9986261-7-8

FIRST PRINTING
Published by Cedar Creek Press, LLC
Boise, Idaho

All rights reserved. No part of this book may be reproduced or transmitted in any form or by any means, electronic or mechanical, including photocopying, recording, or by any information storage and retrieval system, without written permission from Cedar Creek Press, LLC. Brief quotes for the purpose of reviews are allowed.

# DEDICATION

*For Rinda Just*
*First among editors*

# CONTENTS

## SYMBOLS

On Names, Nicknames, Mottos, Potatoes, and Plates ...............5

Can You Spot This Idaho Symbol? ...............11

The Bluebird Probably Not On Your Shoulder ...............13

Idaho Has a Cutthroat Symbol ...............14

Our Decisive Salamander ...............15

Do Si Do ...............16

An Equus is an Equus, Of Course, Of Course ...............17

Idaho's Unique Rock Star ...............18

Our Migrating Monarchs ...............19

"I'm Your Huckleberry" ...............21

The Art Contest Winner We Still Remember ...............23

A Perfect Match ...............26

The Corps of Discovery Discovered This Symbol ...............27

Morley Nelson and Idaho's State Raptor ...............28

## SIGNS

John Margolies ...............34

Idaho's Sky Map ...............35

Chicken Dinner Road ...............37

Coeur d'Alene's "Movie" Motel ...............39

History Along the Highways ................................................................ 40

The Idaho Stop .................................................................................... 42

The Residents of Kellogg Can Take a Joke ........................................ 43

Petrified Watermelons ......................................................................... 44

The Most Comprehensive List of Stinker Station Signs You're Likely to Find ..... 45

Ghostly Lake Hazel ............................................................................. 49

Muffler Men Aren't All Men .............................................................. 50

Just What Are They Protesting? ......................................................... 52

Rock Writing ........................................................................................ 53

The Adelmann Building ..................................................................... 54

The Sampson Roads ............................................................................ 55

The "World Famous" Ranch Club ...................................................... 57

Something's Fishy Here ....................................................................... 59

Gone to the Dogs ................................................................................ 60

You Say Potato .................................................................................... 62

# SONGS

A Revolution in Rock ......................................................................... 67

The Song of the West ......................................................................... 69

A Flight on the Tenuous Connection Redeye ................................... 70

Miss Idaho Makes Good ..................................................................... 72

That Hot. Rod. Lincoln ...................................................................... 73

Idaho in Lyrics ..................................................................................... 75

King of the Road ................................................................................. 77

Idaho's Champagne Lady .................................................................... 79

The Boise Songs .................................................................................81
Some More Tenuous Connections ........................................................83
A Song With a History ..........................................................................84
"The House the Carpenters Built" ..........................................................85
The Absolutely Indisputable Origin of the Hokey Pokey ..........................86
The Governor Did Not Like That Song ...................................................88

# INTRODUCTION, ACKNOWLEDGMENTS, AND EXCUSES

**T**here's no excuse for a book like this. There is, however, a reason. Read on and determine for yourself if my justification meets the high standards of you, the reader.

Alliteration. There you have it. This book is based on the alliteration of its title, that series of sibilants that sneaked stealthily onto the cover.

I write a daily history blog called *Speaking of Idaho*. It has been my plan from the beginning of that effort to roll the posts into a series of books. The blog is sometimes serious; more often simply quirky. Little of what I write will be of use to future historians or current Idaho fourth graders, the class where teachers try to interest students in the history of our state.

Despite their overall eccentricity, it is possible to wrestle my stories into broad categories. For instance, the second book in my series will likely be called *Heroes and Villains*. That category makes sense and will require little explanation. Which reminds me that I'm supposed to be explaining my choice to go with a book based on alliteration.

Here goes. Ready? I like alliteration. Tom Trusky, who was my mentor, cautioned me against its overuse. Did you notice the "acknowledgments" part of the headline above? There you have one. Tom, who was, sadly, born in Oregon, spent most of his life teaching writers at Boise State University. Though that was a noble enough calling, he spent many spare minutes looking for quirky stories about his adopted state. He revived interest in Nell Shipman and her Priest Lake movie studio, and James Castle, deaf-mute king of outsider art. He glorified Idaho potato sacks in art exhibits, taught how to make paper from Idaho materials, exalted Hemingway, made the literary world take notice of BSU's *cold drill* literary magazine, and started the Idaho Center for the Book. If it was quirky and surprising, he labeled it a "treat." It is my hope that he would have found many treats between the pages of this alliteratively titled book, which could have been dedicated to him if I hadn't already done so with my novel, *Keeping Private Idaho*.

If you've read this far, I have tricked you into reading about those who have contributed to this mash-up in ways large and small, including editors Stacey Smekofske and Gretchen Mullins, and book designer Meggan Laxalt Mackey, Studio M Publications & Design. My thanks to the staff at the Idaho State Archives, Boise Arts and History, and Boise State University Special Collections and Archives. I couldn't do what I do if it weren't for the resources of the Boise Public Library! Picky punctuationists please note the name of that library includes an exclamation point. I am also indebted to countless, often nameless, writers at newspapers for penning those first drafts so many years ago and authors of well-researched books whom I have tried to recognize in context as I prattle on.

Finally, reluctantly, I must acknowledge Mark Zuckerberg for creating the imperfect, infuriating, and indispensable platform on which I make my daily appearance. Thanks, Mark. Now quit randomly changing stuff.

# SYMBOLS

# ON NAMES, NICKNAMES, MOTTOS, POTATOES, AND PLATES

**W**hat's in a name? No, I will not go totally Shakespeare on you. This is about Idaho, in particular the name of the state.

When I was in fourth grade, I learned that the word "Idaho" meant "gem of the mountains." It was an Indian word, my teacher said. But Mrs. Adameck was wrong.

Many of us were taught that the name Idaho came from the Indian word "E-Da-How." That Indian word meant "Gem of the Mountains," or "light coming down the mountains," or something similar.

However, researchers say there wasn't a word like that in any Native American language. It turns out the name Idaho was simply invented by someone who thought it sounded Indian.

George M. Willing came up with the word Idaho in 1860. He lobbied to have it become the name for what is now Colorado. He told people it was an Indian word that meant "gem of the mountains." That state might have been called Idaho, but someone discovered the name had been invented. The new territory became Colorado, which means colored or red in Spanish. The nearly name still lingers as the moniker of Idaho Springs, Colorado.

When it came time to name our new territory in 1863, Congress was about to call it Montana, but the name Idaho cropped up again. By that time, the nation's leaders had forgotten that Idaho was a made-up name. An Oregon senator convinced his colleagues to abandon the name Montana because the word meant nothing at all. Idaho, he said, meant "gem of the mountains."

And, the new territory was named Idaho.

Meanwhile, as you may know, the name Montana, which means something like mountainous in Spanish and Latin, was used for another territory.

Through all this it seemed not to occur to anyone why there was a need for a single word that meant "gem of the mountains" in the first place.

So, my fourth-grade teacher wasn't wrong when she told me what Idaho meant. It was the conventional wisdom of the time until renowned Idaho historian Merle Wells discovered the history of the name a few years later. A name that means quite a lot to Idahoans today.

So, now that we knew what to call it, people decided the state also needed a nickname. Often a nickname is shorter than a given name, i.e., Bob is short for Robert, and Jim for James. Given just that parameter, Idaho would probably be called Ida. That didn't ever catch on.

Idaho's nickname grew out of the supposed meaning of the word that George Willing invented. His definition, "gem of the mountains," got shortened to the Gem State. That one stuck. All states have nicknames, but only seven, including Idaho, seem sure enough of themselves to need only one nickname.

Although the name Idaho was considered for three states and had no actual meaning, its purported meaning fit the state well. People have found jasper, opal, jade, topaz, zircon, tourmaline, star garnets, and even diamonds in the Gem State. Some have made the bold claim that every known gemstone can be found in Idaho. There are some 300 gemstones. I'm still waiting to see that 300-stone Idaho collection.

So, now with a name and a nickname, we're ready for business, right? Not quite. Every state has a motto, most of them in Latin. Idaho fell in with the majority, choosing *Esto Perpetua*, or "Let it be perpetual" or "be eternal" as the state motto.

An odd sidebar to this is that Secretary of State George Curtis thought the definition was not quite right, so in 1942 he ran a contest asking citizens to come up with a more "suitable" definition. A 12-year-old girl from Lava Hot Springs, Etheleen E. Evans, wrote a patriotic letter suggesting the definition be "May she be forever under Old Glory." That won the heart of the secretary of state, but it fell flat with the public.

Definitions do change, but one advantage of using the dead Latin language is that it stays much the same as it has been for centuries. This is useful when you want someone who speaks Portuguese and understands Latin to get the meaning of your concept. It doesn't work so well if you want to discuss Tupperware. So, hurray for the first part of that Lava Hot Springs girl's definition. Boo for the second part, patriotic as it may be. There's just nothing about a flag in *Esto Perpetua*.

## SYMBOLS, SIGNS, & SONGS

Which brings us to the state flag of Idaho. Since it is largely the state seal centered on a blue background, one would think we would have had an Idaho state flag for as long as we've had a seal, since 1891. Not so.

It took the Legislature 17 years to pass a law creating an Idaho State Flag. Even then they punted to the adjutant general, delegating the duty of coming up with the design and specifying that the flag would be blue and have the word Idaho on it. They appropriated 100 dollars to make that happen on March 12, 1907.

It seemed odd to me that they put 100 dollars in the adjutant general's budget. Why would he need anything? He could just send a flag company a picture of the state seal and tell them how it was supposed to appear on flags. Voila! Make some flags!

My misunderstanding was that the 100 dollars was for the cost of making a single flag. The state wasn't planning on waving a flag from every courthouse in Idaho. The Legislature had the adjutant general design then order *one* flag.

Idaho got along with a single official state flag for years. It made the headlines in 1926 that the flag was traveling out of state with Governor C.C. Moore so that both could attend the governors' conference in Cheyenne. The stay-at-home flag had only traveled out of state a couple of times before that. It lived in the governor's office when not visiting other states. Today that original flag is in the possession of the Idaho State Historical Society.

*The first Idaho state flag. Photo courtesy of the Idaho State Historical Society.*

# RICK JUST ❦ SPEAKING OF IDAHO HISTORY SERIES ❦

Are we done yet with how we let the world know about this place called Idaho? Not quite. Go read your license plate.

Idaho doesn't have an official slogan, as some states do, but it might as well be "Famous Potatoes," the slogan that graces most Idaho license plates.

A tip of the hat to the Idaho Potato Commission for their tireless efforts to keep that slogan on the plates. Also, a blatting raspberry to the Idaho Potato Commission for their efforts, etc., etc. One can love potatoes and still prefer not to be a rolling advertisement for them. I fall into that camp. Many of us like-minded folks have discovered that certain specialized and personalized plates do not carry the slogan. In the late 1980s, that wasn't the case. I took on the slogan in a way that I hoped would be viewed as humorous by my many friends and family members in Bingham County who raise potatoes.

Potatoes started showing up on Idaho plates in 1948. The slogan on the bottom of the plates that year and the following year was "World Famous Potatoes." In case that was too subtle for you, the silver plates featured a large, full-color baked potato sticker slapped on in the middle of the plate.

The hot potato was dropped in 1950, along with the slogan. The slogan came back in 1953, disappeared in '54 and '55, and came back in '56. In 1957 "World" was dropped from the slogan, making it "Famous Potatoes." That's the slogan that has stuck ever since.

Did I tell you how much I love potatoes? Love 'em. Not so much on my license plates, though. So, in the late 1980s my brother, Kent Just, and I set out to give Idahoans a choice. I located the company that made the reflective material used on the license plates at that time and learned that you could buy it in strips. I ordered a roll of the stuff and had slogans printed on it in the same size, font, and color as the slogan on the license plates. Buyers could peel off the paper on the

## SYMBOLS, SIGNS, & SONGS

back and stick the new slogan over "Famous Potatoes." We sold them for a couple of bucks through Stinker Stations. You could pick from "Famous Potholes," "The Whitewater State," and several others. Kent acted as the front man on this project, because I was working for the State of Idaho at the time and was a little unsure about how my employer would take this little prank. We got publicity for the project in papers from Washington State to Washington, DC. Some articles made it sound like we had a factory cranking these out by the thousands. No. I had a roll of stickers and a pair of scissors.

Kent dropped in on Idaho's attorney general, whom we both knew. We thought we might get a little free advice about the legality of the stickers. The AG, we'll give him the pseudonym of "Jim" to protect the innocent, said to Kent, "You were never here."

Encouraging people to put an unauthorized sticker on a license plate ruffled the feathers of the folks over at Idaho State Police HQ. They made noises about it sufficient to make us stop selling them. We were certain we were on solid legal ground because the US Supreme Court had already ruled that it was legal to cover up a license plate slogan in the name of free speech (New Hampshire's "Live Free or Die"). Still, it didn't seem worthwhile to hire a lawyer for a $150 joke. We'd had our fun, and we'd already made our money back.

Nowadays I'm content to display a potato-free personalized plate, no longer a scofflaw.

# CAN YOU SPOT THIS IDAHO SYMBOL?

Idaho is horse country and has been for over 250 years. Idaho even stakes a claim to a breed, the Appaloosa.

The Appaloosa horse can be traced back to the Mongols in ancient China. It is the oldest identifiable horse breed. It wasn't called the Appaloosa until it became associated with the place later known as Idaho. The horses were well known on the Palouse prairie of northern Idaho, and over the years, those Palouse horses became known as *Appaloosas*.

The spotted horses came to the Northwest through Mexico. Spanish conquistadors lost or traded away enough of them to assure thriving herds in the new world. The Shoshone Tribe had them first, but it was the Nez Perce who perfected the breed.

*Idaho's state horse is the Appaloosa. Not specifically this Appaloosa, though we could do worse. This is a photo of Dreamfinder, an iconic stallion of the breed inducted into the Appaloosa Horse Club Hall of Fame in 1996. Photo courtesy of ApHC.*

## SYMBOLS, SIGNS, & SONGS

Horses gave the Nez Perce an expanded range and produced a whole new way of living for them. They became buffalo hunters and developed trade relationships with other tribes far removed from their traditional range.

The Appaloosa was nearly lost when the great Nez Perce herds were split up and scattered following the Nez Perce War. An ambitious plan to save the horses brought the breed back from near extinction in the 1930s.

Today, thousands of the tough little horses with spotted blankets on their rear quarters can be seen in Idaho and around the world. If you visit Moscow, Idaho, don't miss the Appaloosa Museum, where you can learn the complete story of the breed that became Idaho's State Horse in 1975.

# IDAHO HAS A CUTTHROAT SYMBOL

**I**daho is famous for trout. We raise more trout for restaurants than any other state. Clear Springs Foods in Buhl raises over 20 million pounds of them every year. But it's our equally famous catchable trout that fishermen love.

Idaho Fish and Game stocks over 30 million fish each year in the state's lakes and streams. Most of them are rainbow trout or kokanee salmon.

Our four main native trout include the rainbow, the bull trout, the cutthroat, and the steelhead.

People are most familiar with rainbow trout. Idaho's record rainbow trout was a 20-pound monster caught in the Snake River in 2009.

Unlike the rest of their native trout cousins, steelhead spend part of their life in the ocean, as much as 1800 miles from where they were hatched. Idaho's record steelhead was caught in the Clearwater River in 1973. It weighed just over 30 pounds.

The bull trout, or Dolly Varden, is an even bigger fish. The Idaho record is 32 pounds. That one was caught in Lake Pend Oreille in 1949. It's a record that will stand for a while. It is no longer legal to harvest a bull trout. You can catch them, you just can't keep them.

According to biologists, the first native Idaho trout was a cutthroat that swam into our waters about a million years ago. Cutthroat are very aggressive eaters, so they're easy to catch. The biggest one caught in our state weighed just shy of 19 pounds. It was pulled out of Bear Lake in 1970. The cutthroat—in general, not that specific fish—became Idaho's state fish in 1990.

*You can enjoy Idaho's state fish on your license plate, or on your dinner plate. Displaying the former helps fund the Nongame Wildlife section of Idaho Fish and Game. Management of game animals is funded through the purchase of hunting and fishing licenses.*

# THE BLUEBIRD PROBABLY NOT ON YOUR SHOULDER

In 1931, the Legislature named the mountain bluebird as Idaho's state bird. There are two kinds of bluebirds in Idaho, the western bluebird, and the larger mountain bluebird.

The male mountain bluebird has a bright blue back, a paler blue body, and a whitish belly. The female is a gray-brown bird with a trace of blue on her wings, rump, and tail.

Bluebirds live throughout Idaho in high desert juniper, meadows in forested areas, in mountain valleys, and along open ridges. Most live above 4,000 feet. Their favorite food is the grasshopper. There are plenty of grasshoppers in Idaho for them to eat, but bluebirds have a problem. And you can help.

Bluebirds like to nest in holes that woodpeckers and other animals have excavated. Vacant holes are getting scarce. Many trees with suitable nesting holes have been cut for firewood, burned, or removed for development. The good tree holes that remain are often taken by starlings and sparrows, two non-native species that tend to bully the gentle bluebirds away. That's the bad news. The good news is that bluebirds love to move into a nice, new wooden nesting box that you can provide them. The boxes are easy to build, and the Idaho Fish and Game Department has a free brochure that will tell you how to do it.

They're fussy about where they nest, so if you live in town, don't bother with a box. They like rural areas away from buildings.

*Have you noticed all those non-natives moving into the state? So has the state bird. When I say non-native I'm referring to invasive species such as sparrows and starlings. They tend to take all the good nesting sites away from our mountain bluebirds. You can help by buying a bluebird plate or by building and installing bluebird boxes, if your place is big enough to suit the needs of the bluebirds.*

# OUR DECISIVE SALAMANDER

**I**daho has its share of state symbols, ranging from the Appaloosa horse to the Idaho giant salamander. One can argue about whether we need as many symbols as we have or any at all. I will stay away from that one.

It offers a good excuse to talk about an amazing creature that is found almost nowhere else. The Idaho giant salamander lives only in Idaho and in a small area of western Montana. It's a giant only in comparison with other salamanders, coming in at about 13 inches. It can be found in streams and rivers doing mostly what it does best, eating. It has a voracious appetite, but as long as you have a spine you're not likely prey. They eat mostly invertebrates.

Idaho giant salamanders are incredible animals and are best known for one peculiar trick. Most of them live their lives in streams scarfing down snails and such, but a small percentage of them find life on land a better gig. It's not that they go back and forth. They're either stream dwellers that have the necessary gills for that (right below), or they live out their life on land, losing their gills and developing lungs (left below, photos by Dr. John Cossel, Jr.). The land-dwelling salamanders develop a different, more upright body stance. Their head changes shape and their eyes take up a new position. Even their color changes. Most people looking at a stream-dweller and a land-dweller together would swear they were completely different species.

The Idaho giant salamander became Idaho's official amphibian in 2015, following five years of lobbying efforts by persistent Idaho teen Ilah Hickman. To learn more about the Idaho giant salamander, Google "Windows on Wildlife Giant Salamander."

*Idaho giant salamanders have a decision to make. Do they want to spend their lives wagging along through the water, or would they rather hotfoot it onto land? We don't know how or why they make that decision, or if it is really a decision and not something in their environment that pulls the trigger. The salamander on the left grew lungs and ventured onto the land for its habitat. The salamander on the right kept its gills and stayed in the water. Once the decision is made, they can't change their mind. Or whatever it is that changes.*

# DO SI DO

Our state's claim to the "Hokey Pokey" aside (see page 86), the dance was snubbed when in 1989 the Legislature declared Idaho's official state dance the square dance. It came out of the Senate Commerce and Labor Committee with a "Do Pass—with enthusiasm!" recommendation.

The National Folk-Dance Committee tried to make the square dance the official national dance in 1988, without success. As often happens when something fails on the national level, the group aimed their sights at the states. Idaho couldn't resist the lobbyists from Big Dance. It became one of 19 states to decide, suddenly, that it just had to have a state dance.

I dance only in the shower, so have not participated in this particular passion. I am told that the name comes from the beginning placement of couples. Two face each other, let's say, north and south, and two east and west. In the American version of the dance, a caller calls out instructions to the dancers while the music plays. Apparently, without revulsion, the couples do-si-do on command.

The square dance has its roots in 16th-century England, though it has become strongly associated with Western—as in cowboy Western—culture. When the bill to make it the state dance was introduced, Idaho Senator Claire Wetherell, (D for Democrat and Dance) said, "Square dancing is typical of Idaho's lifestyle." Well, okay. I'm not sure I can get seven other people in the shower, though.

# AN EQUUS IS AN EQUUS, OF COURSE, OF COURSE

**T**he Hagerman Horse, so named by locals, was discovered in 1928. Scientists call it *Equus simplicidens*. Five nearly complete skeletons and 100 skulls were retrieved from a hillside across the Snake River near the town of Hagerman. Some paleontologists speculate that a herd of the horses may have been caught in flooding waters and drowned at the site. The Hagerman site remains the largest single discovery of this fossil found, and it is the earliest example of Equus, the genus that includes all modern horses, donkeys, and zebras. Even Mr. Ed.

It's not all about the horses at the Hagerman site. Preserved within the sediments is one of the most diverse deposits of Pliocene animals. Over 100 species of vertebrates, including 18 fish, four amphibians, nine reptiles, 27 birds, and 50 mammals have been identified, as well as freshwater snails, clams, and plant pollen.

Idaho Department of Parks and Recreation owned and operated the site for a few years. It was traded for land that became Castle Rocks State Park in 2003. The National Park Service operates the site today as Hagerman Fossil Beds National Monument.

Not every state has a state fossil, but Idaho does. It is a horse, of course, of course, the Hagerman Horse, named the state fossil in 1988.

*This photo from 1968, shows Bob Romig, curator of collections at the Idaho State Historical Society examining the skeleton of what is probably Idaho's most famous fossil. The Hagerman Horse was a zebra-like creature about the size of a present-day Arabian horse.* Idaho Statesman *photo.*

# IDAHO'S UNIQUE ROCK STAR

**T**he Gem State's best-known gemstone is the star garnet. Garnets are usually a dark purple or plum color. Some call the stone "red gold."

Garnets are not especially rare. They're commonly found in metamorphic rocks. However, star garnets are rare. They have been discovered in only two places on earth, India and Idaho. That's why the 1967 Idaho legislature made the star garnet the official state gem stone.

Most star garnets have four rays that seem to shimmer and float across the surface of the polished stone as it's moved in the light. But the rarest of the rare have six rays or arms in the star. Collectors covet the beautiful six-ray garnet—found only in northern Idaho.

You can dig for star garnets yourself, if you're the adventurous type. You're likely to be digging somewhere near Emerald Creek, so named because… garnets. Apparently, someone thought the reddish gems were emeralds. The digging is regulated by the Forest Service, and it requires an inexpensive permit. You can even hire an outfitter who will guarantee you find at least one cuttable garnet. The Moscow Chamber of Commerce can give you information. Maybe you'll be lucky enough to find a rare six-ray star garnet. There's not much point looking anywhere else but Idaho.

# OUR MIGRATING MONARCHS

**D**id you know Idaho has a state insect? Yes, as do 44 other states. Many of them have two state insects, so stand by for legislation.

Idaho's state insect is the monarch butterfly made official in 1992. Monarchs get around, so it may not surprise you that it is also the state insect of Vermont, Texas, Minnesota, Illinois, West Virginia, and Alabama.

Monarchs, or *Danaus plexippus*, if you want to get all Latin, rely on milkweed in their larval stage. As adult butterflies, they feed on a variety of nectar-producing plants, accidentally spreading around pollen at the same time.

*Monarch butterflies, Idaho's state insect, spend summers in Idaho and migrate to southern California for the winter. Photo by Allen Dale.*

You probably know that monarchs migrate south for the winter. Western monarchs, those found in Idaho, typically over-winter in southern California, mostly around Pacific Grove. It's not the same butterfly coming back in the spring that you waved farewell to in October. It takes three or four generations of butterflies to make a migration loop.

Many Idahoans can identify a monarch caterpillar. Or, can you? It surprised me to learn that there are a series of five stages of growth for a monarch in the larval form. The first caterpillar to hatch from those tiny butterfly eggs is translucent green, and less than a quarter of an inch long. It eats ferociously, then molts, revealing the beginnings of the white, black, and yellow markings we are familiar with.

## SYMBOLS, SIGNS, & SONGS

It eats again, and molts again, etc., until it reaches the fifth and final stage and its ultimate size, about two inches long.

An adult monarch is a distinctive orange with black branching stripes leading to black wing edges with a double outline of white dots. If you see one that looks significantly smaller than you'd expect (a wingspan of about 3.5 to 4 inches), it's not a baby butterfly (no such thing). It's probably a viceroy butterfly.

Milkweed, which is unfortunately often considered a weed, is essential in the life-cycle of the monarch. So, if you can let the plants grow, you'll be helping Idaho's official insect.

# "I'M YOUR HUCKLEBERRY"

According to Victoria Wilcox, who has done way more research on the topic than I have the patience for, the phrase "I'm your huckleberry" has a proud literary tradition. Walter Noble Burns used the 19th century slang phrase in his 1927 novel, *Tombstone: The Iliad of the Southwest*. It was an early novel about the Earp brothers and Doc Holliday. The phrase means something like, "I'm the man for the job" or "I'm your hero." Val Kilmer uttered the same phrase in the 1993 movie *Tombstone*, which was based on the aforementioned book and the screenplay written by Kevin Jarre. A contemporary homage of the phrase can be found in the multi-player first shooter game *Overwatch*.

This is a roundabout way of putting a little meat on the bones of this story about Idaho's state fruit, the huckleberry. What else is there to say about huckleberries, except, "Yum"?

That luscious taste aside, huckleberry is a funny name. The friendly ghosts at *Wikipedia* tell us the name is "a North American variation of the English dialectal name variously called 'hurtleberry' or 'whortleberry,'" as if that explains anything.

*Val Kilmer may not have known it was a reference to Idaho's state fruit when he uttered the words, "I'm your huckleberry" while playing Doc Holliday in the 1993 movie "Tombstone." The antiquated phrase has enjoyed something of a resurgence since then. You can buy any number of t-shirts with that line artistically printed on them. Some like huckleberries (or maybe just that quote) so much that they've had it tattooed on their bodies.*

## SYMBOLS, SIGNS, & SONGS

Huckle, hurtle, whortle, or whatever you'd like to call it, the berry became Idaho's official state fruit in 2000 when the combined fourth and fifth grade class at Southside Elementary in Cocolalla convinced their legislators to introduce a bill to that effect. Cocolalla, Idaho is on Cocolalla Lake, about 13 miles south of Sandpoint, close to the heart of huckleberry country. So, if you were hankering for Idaho's state fruit and wanted a personal guide to the best picking area, you could ask about any of the residents if they would be your huckleberry. Chances are good they wouldn't strike you, but you'll get some raised eyebrows. Also, they will not tell you where to pick.

# THE ART CONTEST WINNER
# WE STILL REMEMBER

**T**he great seal of the State of Idaho was approved in 1891 and can be found on business cards, letterheads, brochures, proclamations, and other official state documents. It is also the centerpiece of Idaho's flag.

Emma Edwards Green, who was born in California and was the daughter of a former governor of Missouri, was teaching art classes in Boise when the brand-new Idaho Legislature announced a contest to design a state seal. She entered the competition and won 100 dollars. To this day, it remains the only state seal designed by a woman.

Green got much input regarding the seal. She wrote,

> "Before designing the seal, I was careful to make a thorough study of the resources and future possibilities of the State. I invited the advice and counsel of every member of the Legislature and other citizens qualified to help in creating a Seal of State that really represented Idaho at that time."

*The $100 she won for designing Idaho's state seal did not make Emma Edwards Green wealthy, but it did bring her a measure of lasting fame. She is the only woman to have designed a state seal.*

## SYMBOLS, SIGNS, & SONGS

Green also gave it a lot of thought, writing the following:

> The question of Woman Suffrage was being agitated somewhat, and as leading men and politicians agreed that Idaho would eventually give women the right to vote, and as mining was the chief industry, and the mining man the largest financial factor of the state at that time, I made the figure of the man the most prominent in the design, while that of the woman, signifying justice, as noted by the scales; liberty, as denoted by the liberty cap on the end of the spear, and equality with man as denoted by her position at his side, also signifies freedom. The pick and shovel held by the miner, and the ledge of rock beside which he stands, as well as the pieces of ore scattered about his feet, all indicate the chief occupation of the State. The stamp mill in the distance, which you can see by using a magnifying glass, is also typical of the mining interest of Idaho. The shield between the man and woman is emblematic of the protection they unite in giving the state. The large fir or pine tree in the foreground in the shield refers to Idaho's immense timber interests.
> The husbandman plowing on the left side of the shield, together with the sheaf of grain beneath the shield, are emblematic of Idaho's agricultural resources, while the cornucopias, or horns of plenty, refer to the horticultural. Idaho has a game law, which protects the elk and moose. The elk's head, therefore, rises above the shield. The state flower, the wild Syringa or Mock Orange, grows at the woman's feet, while the ripened wheat grows as high as her shoulder. The star signifies a new light in the galaxy of states… The river depicted in the shield is our mighty Snake or Shoshone River, a stream of great majesty.

In regard to the coloring of the emblems used in the making of the Great Seal of the State of Idaho, my principal desire was to use such colors as would typify pure Americanism and the history of the State. As Idaho was a virgin state, I robed my goddess in white and made the liberty cap on the end of the spear the same color. In representing the miner, I gave him the garb of the period suggested by such mining authorities as former United States Senator George Shoup, of Idaho, former Governor Norman B. Willey of Idaho, former Governor James H. Hawley of Idaho, and other mining men and early residents of the state who knew intimately the usual garb of the miner. Almost unanimously they said, "Do not put the miner in a red shirt. Make the shirt a grayish brown," said Captain J.J. Wells, chairman of the Seal Committee. The "Light of the Mountains" is typified by the rosy glow which precedes the sunrise.

If that sounds a little busy to you, you would not be alone. The state seal was updated in 1957 to simplify it a bit, though it remains, let's say, hard working.

# A PERFECT MATCH

This Idaho state symbol is probably in your kitchen cupboard right now. The western white pine is an important tree for the timber industry. It's a durable, close-grained tree that is uniform in texture.

White pine is lightweight, seasons without warping, takes nails without splitting, and saws easily. That makes it a terrific tree for door and window frames, cabinets, and paneling. Oh yes, about the white pine that's in your cupboard right now—kitchen matches.

The western white pine does best in a cool and dry climate. Although it can grow at sea level, it prefers elevations of 2500 to 6000 feet. In Idaho, it grows mostly in the panhandle. A mature tree typically gets to be about 100 feet high.

A gregarious tree, the western white pine seems to prefer mixing with other common evergreens rather than in large stands of its own. One plant it would be better off not mixing with is the currant. A fungus called pine blister rust kills the pine, but it's only found where currants or gooseberries grow.

The western white pine was named the state tree of Idaho by the 1935 Legislature.

*This photo is labeled as the "Largest Known White Pine." How large? It was 207 feet tall and its diameter was 6-feet 7-inches. It scaled at 29,800 board feet measure. The rings counted out at 425, so it was 425 years old when cut down in 1912. The live tree was located seven miles northwest of Bovill. Photo courtesy of the Idaho State Historical Society, 78-37-158.*

# THE CORPS OF DISCOVERY DISCOVERED THIS SYMBOL

The Lewis and Clark expedition discovered not only Idaho but the Idaho state flower. In 1806, Captain Meriwether Lewis discovered and collected the first specimen of syringa. The shrub's scientific name, *Philadelphus lewisii*, recognizes that fact.

Of course, the plant wasn't new to the Indians. They had used it for generations, making soap from the leaves and arrows from the stems.

Syringa is a beautiful plant. The shrub grows from 3 to 12 feet high and features large clusters of white flowers with bright yellow stamens. A hillside covered with syringa in the spring can look almost like a snowfield. It would be hard to miss a big patch of the plant, even blindfolded. Syringa gives off a strong orange aroma. Many people call it mock orange.

You'll find syringa growing along streams and on hillsides to near 7,000 feet. It often grows along with chokecherry and serviceberry. One indicator of a large deer population is a stand of syringa that has been heavily browsed, because the animals normally prefer other foods.

Another likely candidate for the honor of state flower might have been Clarkia, which is in the primrose family. Captain William Clark discovered it along Idaho's Clearwater River. Syringa became Idaho's state flower in 1931.

# MORLEY NELSON AND IDAHO'S STATE RAPTOR

Idaho is a mecca for raptor lovers from all over the world. That's because it is a magnet for birds of prey. The World Center for Birds of Prey is in Boise. Boise State University is home to the Raptor Research Center and offers the only Masters of Science in Raptor Biology, and The Morley Nelson Snake River Birds of Prey National Conservation Area (NCA) is south of Kuna.

The birds congregate in the NCA not because it is a protected area, but because it is an ideal place for raptors to live. The uplift of air from the Snake River Canyon makes flying and gliding a breeze for the birds. The uplands above the canyon rim provide habitat for ground squirrels and other critters the birds consider lunch.

Morley Nelson first saw the canyon in the late 1940s. He had developed a love for raptors—especially peregrine falcons—growing up on a farm in North Dakota. When he moved to Idaho, following a WWII stint with the famous Tenth Mountain Division, he went out to the Snake River Canyon to see if he could find some raptors. He found a few. There are typically about 800 pairs of hawks, eagles, owls, and falcons that nest there each spring. It's the greatest concentration of nesting raptors in North America, and probably the world.

Nelson became evangelical about the birds and their Snake River Canyon habitat. He worked on films about the birds with Walt Disney, Paramount Pictures, the Public Broadcasting System, and others. His passion for raptors was contagious, and through his efforts, public understanding of their role in the natural world was greatly enhanced.

Morley Nelson convinced Secretary of the Interior Rogers Morton to establish the Snake River Birds of Prey Natural Area in 1971.

He lobbied Interior Secretary Cecil Andrus to expand the area in 1980. Then in 1993, US Representative Larry LaRocco led an effort in Congress to designate some 485,000 acres of the canyon and uplands as a National Conservation Area.

It was also Nelson who led the effort to convince the Peregrine Fund to relocate to Boise and build the World Center for Birds of Prey south of town. Today, peregrines have recovered thanks to the center's captive breeding program and other efforts.

*Morley Nelson with one of his favorite birds, a gyrfalcon named Thor. Photo courtesy of Steve Stuebner.*

The World Center for Birds of Prey now concentrates on programs to save the aplomado falcon and the California condor.

While efforts to recover peregrines were going on, Nelson led a pioneering effort to save raptors from power line electrocution. He worked with the Edison Electric Institute and Idaho Power to study how raptors used the manmade perches known as power poles. Because of that research, poles are now designed to minimize electrocution and even provide safe nesting areas for the birds.

Morley lived to see Idaho become the only state to have a state raptor. Thanks to the hard work of a group of fourth graders, the peregrine falcon became the state raptor in 2004.

When Morley Nelson passed away in 2005, he had unquestionably done more to save and protect raptors than any other single person.

For more on Morley Nelson, see his biography, *Cool North Wind*, written by Steve Stuebner.

# SIGNS

# SIGNS

**T**his section of the book started out as a tip of the hat to highway signs, but I soon ran the thing off the road. I kept expanding the definition of "sign" and before you knew it, I was including a bunch of rocks and a giant dog. I might more accurately call it "Things That Catch Your Attention When You're Driving in Idaho." That seems a little long, so, "Signs" it is.

# JOHN MARGOLIES

John Margolies was an architectural critic who set out to capture iconic vernacular architecture and signs across the United States through his photographs. He loved the cheesy roadside attractions that often made no pretense of skillful design. He is also credited with bringing many historic buildings to the attention of people who might not have recognized their architectural value. As a result, many of them are today on the National Register of Historic Places. The Library of Congress began collecting his images in 2007, and they are made available today to researchers and writers of goofy little books. Several of the photos used in this section are courtesy of the Library of Congress *John Margolies Roadside America Photograph Archive*. Each is identified within the caption or with the word Margolies following the caption.

*(1) Rio Theater, 1980, 271 Broadway in Idaho Falls, opened as the Broadway Theater in 1928 and was renamed the Rio in 1934. Today it's the ARTitorium, operated by Idaho Falls Arts Council. (2) Winchester's Cadilac (sic) Ranch sign beckons travelers to pull off US-95 for food and fuel. Lest you think this might not be as classy as it seems, the Cadilac (sic) is Pepto Bismol pink. (3) Silver Dragon restaurant sign, Coeur d'Alene. It is a classic, right down to the Chinese-ish lettering of "Foods," 1987. (4) Paul Bunyan Pak-Out sign in Coeur d'Alene (5) The Chief Hotel in Cascade sports an iconic sign of an Indian chief in a war bonnet, 2004. (6) Evergreen Gables Motel, Idaho Falls, 1977. The sign still exists, but it is in serious need of some love. Photos courtesy of John Margolies Roadside America photograph archive (1972-2008), Library of Congress, Prints and Photographs Division.*

# IDAHO'S SKY MAP

Most highways in Idaho have regular markers indicating speed limits, impending crashes if you fail to stop, and the mileage to the next three towns. That's all very handy, but what if you're commuting by air? Nowadays, with sophisticated navigational equipment, getting around in an airplane is something akin to that map app on your phone, speaking to you in a calm voice while you yell at it. In earlier days of airplanes, getting around was more flying by the seat of your pants; a cliché which owes its existence to flying.

A pilot could easily get a bit off course and think the town below her was Rigby when it was really Rexburg. So, airmarking was invented. In 1934, Phoebe F. Omlie, Special Assistant for Air Intelligence of the National Advisory Committee for Aeronautics, convinced the Bureau of Air Commerce to start a program whereby each state would mark their towns and cities so they could be seen from the air. Mind that there is an additional hierarchy of names and acronyms associated with the program from which I've just saved you. You're welcome.

Note that our fictional pilot attempting to discern Rigby from Rexburg in the example above was female. That's a little nod to the airmarking project being the first US government program, "Conceived, planned, and directed by a woman with an all-woman staff," according to the website of the Ninety-Nines, the leading organization of woman pilots.

The idea was to paint the name of a town on the roof of a building in bright yellow paint and outlined in black. Idaho took part in the program. It was successful. Too successful, in some locations. During WWII, officials determined that it was not such a good idea to provide enemy bombers with a "You are here" locater. The program quickly switched from painting town names on warehouse roofs to painting over town names on warehouse roofs, at least in coastal states. After the war, the paint switched from black back to yellow.

Every town in Idaho that had a roof big enough for letters got its 20-foot-high sign. Typically, the State Department of Aeronautics hired a college crew during the summer to paint the whole state every five years or so. In 1963, they divided the state into three regions and completed one region a year.

# SYMBOLS, SIGNS, & SONGS

In addition to the town name, a symbol pointed to the nearest airport, and a numeral indicated how far away it was. Some symbols pointed to a couple of nearby airports.

The state no longer runs the program, but as recently as 2005, the Idaho Chapter of the Ninety-Nines was keeping some rooftop signs in good repair.

A related project, accomplished with the Forest Service, marked every Forest Service lookout in Idaho with a number. Again, it was to provide pilots with navigational aids. In 1963, Kenneth Dougal, a college student from Boise, was contracted to paint every lookout in Idaho north of the Salmon River. It entailed driving a panel truck to the top of a mountain, slapping on some big numbers, and winding his way down the mountain toward the next lookout. He painted 110 lookouts and microwave tower buildings. To accomplish this feat, he flew 160 miles by helicopter, rode a horse 92 miles, walked 75 miles, rode a tote-goat (an early, not very sophisticated off highway motorbike) 45 miles, and drove a panel truck eight thousand miles.

This little tidbit of information is courtesy of the October 1963 *Rudder Flutter*, the official publication of the Idaho Department of Aeronautics. That department is now the Division of Aeronautics in the Idaho Department of Transportation. My thanks to Airport Planning and Development Manager Bill Statham and Administrative Assistant Tammy Schoen for providing me with a wealth of information on this subject.

*Every town had an airmarker. Most still do. This photo from the 40s shows the campus of Albion Normal School in Albion with an airmarker on Bocock Hall, the building that once housed the campus theater. Note the arrow indicating the distance to the nearest airport. Photo courtesy of the Idaho Transportation Department Archives maintained by the Idaho State Historical Society.*

# CHICKEN DINNER ROAD

**C**hicken dinner. Yum. It was yummy enough to get a road in Canyon County paved once.

The story about how Chicken Dinner Road got its name appeared in the *Idaho Press Tribune* in about 1992 and reprinted in 2008. It seems that Morris and Laura Lamb were friends of Governor C. Ben Ross and his wife Edna. They ate dinner together many times at the Lamb home.

One day, in the 1930s, Mrs. Lamb, who was renowned for her chicken, rolls, and apple pie meals, was in Boise. She invited the governor to come to dinner. During that conversation, she complained to Ross about the pitiful condition of the road in front of their place which was dirt pocked with potholes. Ross was purported to say something like, "Laura, if you get that road graded and graveled, I'll see to it it's oiled."

Mrs. Lamb approached the Canyon County Commissioners who saw that opportunity as a fine one. They graded and graveled the road. As soon as that was done, she was on the phone to the governor, reminding him of his promise. The story goes that the next day the road was oiled which seems unlikely, but it's Mrs. Lamb's story.

"Chicken Dinner Road" is also the name of a progressive blues band from Boise. From left to right are LB Robertson, John Blakley, Dennis Stokes, Rue Frisbee, Slim Eller.

## SYMBOLS, SIGNS, & SONGS

The story got around and local hooligans thought it would be droll to put up a big hand-scrawled sign in front of the Lamb house in the dark of night. It read, "Lamb's Chicken Dinner Avenue." Mrs. Lamb was not amused. Still, the name stuck as Chicken Dinner Road.

*Idaho Press Tribune* writer Dave Wilkins penned the original story.

And the story continues. In 2019 Tracy Reiman, vice president of People for the Ethical Treatment of Animals (PETA), wrote a letter to Nampa Mayor Garret Nancolas asking him to please rename the road. Their news release said that, "PETA is asking Mayor Nancolas to change this road's name to one that celebrates chickens as individuals, not as beings to kill, chop up, and label as 'dinner.'" The letter was packed with puns such as "ruffle any feathers," "eggciting" idea and "hatch a plan."

The letter got media play for a few days then faded away. The PETA-offending road is in the county, not within the City of Nampa, so there's no point in calling Mayor Nancolas chicken for not changing the name.

# COEUR D'ALENE'S "MOVIE" MOTEL

If you've seen the 1960 Alfred Hitchcock movie, *Psycho*, starring Janet Leigh, you probably shudder every time you step into a motel shower. That stabbing music—and that stabbing—tend to pierce the brain.

An entrepreneur in Coeur d'Alene either took advantage of the movie's fame by naming his lodging site the Bates Motel, or he was named Bates (possibly Randy Bates) and simply took advantage of the coincidence. Readers in Coeur d'Alene will have their opinions.

Be that as it may, any connection to the movie, or the more recent TV series named *Bates Motel*, is tangential at best. There is a rumor, retold endlessly in blurbs such as this one, that Robert Bloch, the man who wrote the book *Psycho* once stayed at the motel. Good luck chasing that down. Another rumor asserts that the very *Psycho*-like sign that for years encouraged people to spend the night was made by a movie production company and later used the movie motel for a movie. Maybe they just stayed there.

Gosh, what if they stayed in room one or room three? Did the ashtrays move inexplicably? Did they feel a chill in the air?

Yes, the other thing the Bates Motel was famous for was its alleged haunting. Rooms one and three held most of the hauntings. There doesn't seem to be a death associated with the hauntings, so it could just be random ghosts, I guess.

Allegedly, the old motel was originally the officers' quarters at the Farragut Naval Training Station. Maybe so. Many old buildings in the area started out there, so that's not far-fetched.

About the only thing we can say for sure about the Bates Motel, once at 2018 E. Sherman Ave., is that it is no longer called that. It's currently the Lighthouse. No word on whether or not the ghosts moved out in disgust when the name changed.

# HISTORY ALONG THE HIGHWAYS

Idaho has one of the best historical highway marker programs in the country, thanks to the continued efforts of the Idaho Transportation Department and the Idaho State Historical Society. If there's a single person to thank, Merle Wells fits the bill.

Dr. Wells started working on the program in the mid-1950s, identifying important sites and writing the text for the signs. The remarkable thing is that he kept the text on each sign to fewer than a hundred words, and he *still* provided a meaningful history lesson. I've used that many words up to this point.

Read what he packed into this marker on U.S. 95 at White Bird Hill.

A Gatling gun, firing from the top of a low hill a mile northwest of here, beat off a Nez Perce attack, July 4, 1877.

The next day, Indians just east of here surrounded 17 Mount Idaho Volunteers: two were killed and three wounded before cavalrymen from Cottonwood came out to rescue them. Meanwhile, Chief Joseph's people, screened by this well-planned diversionary skirmish, crossed the prairie to join their allies on the Clearwater. From there the Indians retired across the mountains to Montana, where the Nez Perce War ended three months later.

*(1) Thanks in large part to Merle Wells, who wrote most of the copy for them, Idaho has a terrific set of historical markers. The 1961 Idaho Transportation Department promotional photo shows Linda Bain and Bill Harvey who got all dressed up, as one does, to stand in the dirt and smell the sage while casually admiring a new sign near Boise. (2) 1947 historic marker, US 30 southeast of Boise. By 1990, when the department published their* Idaho Highway Historical Marker Guide *(sadly now out of print), there were 232 markers*

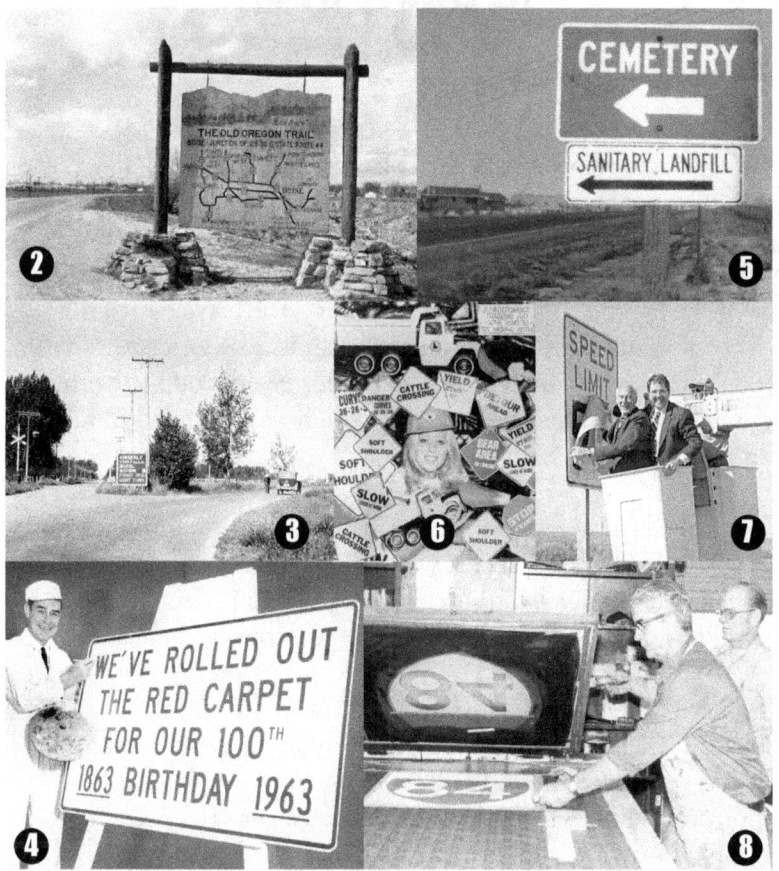

scattered across the state. Merle Wells had written most of them. (3) This helpful sign was put up by the town of Kimberly. The 1925 Idaho Transportation Department photo is tagged "luring traffic into town." Ah ha! You actually can take that turn if you don't mind missing the wonders of Kimberly. (4) Governor Robert E. Smylie pretends to paint a sign welcoming visitors to Idaho during the Territorial Centennial. (5) We don't know where in Idaho this unfortunate pairing on a post took place. The photo is courtesy of the Idaho Department of Transportation where someone had the good sense to save it in their archives for posterity. (6) This display photo from the 1950s was labeled "maintenance training." This should have been followed up with a six-week gender sensitivity course, but it probably wasn't. Did I mention this was in the 1950s? Courtesy of the Idaho Transportation Department, which will likely now burn the negatives. (7) It was a big dang deal when Governor Cecil Andrus and Senator Steve Symms put up the first 65 mph sticker on a 55 mph sign in 1987, providing a rare point of agreement for the Democratic governor and Republican senator. (8) I-84 wasn't always termed an interstate. Parts of it were designated Idaho State Highway 2 for a time and Route A of the Sampson Trails system before that. When the Interstate Highway was conceived in 1956, it was going to be designated I-82. By the time it was actually built the bureaucrats in charge of numbering national highways designated it I-80N. That was changed in 1977 when it became I-84. The unidentified sign makers worked for the Idaho Transportation Department, which provided the photo.

# THE IDAHO STOP

**B**icycles have been in Idaho since territorial days. Unlike horse-drawn conveyances, bikes were not replaced by automobiles.

In May 1911, the *Boise Evening Capital News* was effusive about the future of the bicycle. "No question about it—the bicycle is coming into its own again. Its fine record in the war, its many-sided utility in modern business, its wonderful influence for health coupled with its undoubted economy and convenience—all have combined to make it even more desirable than before."

A.P. Tyler, the local Firestone dealer, was enthusiastic about bicycles and the *Non-Skid* tires Firestone was selling. "I look for a big year for the bicycle trade generally. [Bicycles] meet a distinct need in our modern life—as the only really practical self-propelled vehicle."

Fast forward to 1982 when Idaho showed its love for bicycles in a unique way. The Legislature was revising traffic rules that year and decided to stop cluttering up judicial calendars with "technical violations" of traffic control devices, i.e. stop signs. That was the invention of a law that has become known as the Idaho Stop. Bike riders in Idaho can treat a stop sign the same way drivers treat a yield sign. If the coast is clear, they can roll right through it. A later revision to Idaho code made it legal for bike riders to treat a stop light the same way vehicle drivers treat a stop sign: Stop, check to see if the way is clear, then proceed.

Several other jurisdictions across the country have tried implementing the Idaho Stop for bicyclists. To date, Idaho is the only place it is legal statewide.

# THE RESIDENTS OF KELLOGG CAN TAKE A JOKE

If you check the Kellogg Chamber of Commerce website, you'll find a sophisticated presentation about their town, including photos of happy hikers, the gondola, ATV riders, golfers, and skiers. If you type the word "jackass" into their search engine, you get "no results found." Sad.

Okay, maybe not sad. Certainly, a different approach than they once took, though. The Kellogg Chamber once maintained a sign on the outskirts of town that was all about the jackass and its descendants. The sign read, "You are now near Kellogg. The town which was discovered by a JACKASS—and which is inhabited by its descendants."

The story goes back to before Kellogg was a town. The town was originally called Milo Creek, but in 1887 it was changed to honor Noah Kellogg, the man who discovered a rich vein of ore near there in 1885.

Kellogg, the prospector, had one jackass and a grubstake of $18.75. His jackass strayed away, and when Noah caught up with it, the animal was grazing on an outcropping of galena that seemed promising. Yeah. Something like 30 million tons of lead, silver, and zinc came out of the mines in the valley. So far.

Kellogg is said to have credited the jackass with the discovery so that he didn't have to share the wealth with the folks who had grubstaked him. Courts didn't buy that argument, and the partners got their share. In the end, the jackass may have been better off than his owner who sold the beast. The story goes that the jackass spent his waning years happily grazing away, while Kellogg squandered his money and ended up in poverty.

# PETRIFIED WATERMELONS

In doing research for my book *Fearless—Farris Lind, the Man Behind the Skunk*, I was surprised to learn the origin of the geological term "melon gravel." The scientific designation came about because of one of Farris Lind's Stinker Station signs. It was probably his most famous sign. Erected near Bliss, it sat in a field of lava rocks tumbled and smoothed by the Bonneville Flood. Gus Roos, Lind's sign maker, planted a sign that said, "Petrified Watermelons —Take One Home to Your Mother-In-Law!" Roos painted a few rocks green to complete the effect.

People did stop and pick up rocks for souvenirs, some of them weighing a hundred pounds. Roos went back more than once to paint up more rocks.

One man who stopped to look at the rocks was named Harold E. Malde. He happened to be a geologist. He was so intrigued by the sign, the rocks, and the idea of petrified watermelons that he mentioned it in *Geological Survey Professional Paper 596*. The paper is about the impact of the Bonneville Flood. In it he said, "In 1955, amused by a whimsical billboard that advertised one patch of boulders as 'petrified watermelons,' we applied to them the descriptive geological name Melon Gravel, which has since become one of the many evocative terms in stratigraphic nomenclature" (Malde and Poweres, 1962 p. 1216).

# THE MOST COMPREHENSIVE LIST OF STINKER STATION SIGNS YOU'RE LIKELY TO FIND

 y apologies to digital communicators for the following list. I am *not* yelling at you. The original Stinker Station signs were in all caps, so they are reproduced here that way.

### LIST OF SIGNS

AIN'T THIS MONOTONOUS?
ANY STRANGE TRACK FOUND IN THIS AREA
   BELONGS TO THE UNION PACIFIC
ARE YOU CRAZY ABOUT IDAHO?
   WE HAVE ALL SIZES OF STRAIGHT JACKETS
BE A THINKER — SEE THE STINKER
BEWARE OF CURVES AND SOFT SHOULDERS
BEWARE — IDAHO IS FULL OF LONELY BEAUTIFUL WOMEN
CALIFORNIANS MUST BE DIPPED BEFORE ENTERING IDAHO
CATTLE COUNTRY — WATCH OUT FOR BUM STEERS
DO NOT FEED DESERT RATS
DO YOU HAVE A RESERVATION, OR AREN'T YOU AN INDIAN?
DO YOU HAVE ROCKS IN YOUR HEAD? GET REFILLS HERE
DO YOU SMELL SOMETHING AWFUL? SO DO WE!
DOES YOUR PAROLE BOARD KNOW YOU'RE HERE?
DON'T JUST SIT THERE — NAG YOUR HUSBAND
DON'T WASH YOUR BRITCHES IN FARMER'S DITCHES
DRIVE AT NIGHT — THERE'S MORE MOONSHINE THEN
DRIVE CAREFULLY — THERE'S NO FUTURE IN SUICIDE
DURING RAINY SEASON WATCH OUT FOR COWSLIPS
   AND BULRUSHES
FARM GIRLS ARE NOT PRAIRIE CHICKENS
   (OR DRY FARM TOMATOES)
FISHERMEN BEWARE OF LOAN SHARKS
FISHERMEN — DO YOU HAVE WORMS?
FOR A FAST PICKUP PASS A STATE PATROLMAN
GET YOUR RADIOACTIVE RATTLESNAKES
   AT FAGAN'S PET SHOP

## SYMBOLS, SIGNS, & SONGS

GRIZZLY BEAR FEEDING GROUNDS.
   COUNT YOUR CHILDREN, WATCH YOUR HONEY
HAVE TEA WITH ME — BRING YOUR OWN BAG
HISTERICAL MARKER — CHIEF SACATABACA
   STARVED TO DEATH HERE
HISTERICAL MARKER — WASHINGTON SLEPT HERE*
   *SO DID OREGON
IDAHO'S SKUNKS ARE NOT TO BE SNIFFED AT
IDAHO'S STRONGEST ANIMAL — THE SKUNK
IF YOU LIVED HERE YOU'D BE HOME NOW
IF YOUR WIFE WANTS TO DRIVE,
   DON'T STAND IN HER WAY
INDIANS MUST NOT SCALP TOURISTS WITHIN
   300 FEET OF HIGHWAY
IS YOUR CLUTCH SLIPPING? LET US CHECK YOUR
   REAR END
IT'S LUCKY YOU HAVE FRIENDS OR YOU'DE
   BE A TOTAL STRANGER
IT'S UNCANNY — NO REST ROOMS IN THIS AREA
LET THERE BE A MINUTE OF SILENCE WHILE
   WE CHANGE BACK SEAT DRIVERS
LET US CHECK YOUR BAGGAGE FOR STOLEN TOWELS
LONELY HEARTS CLUB PICNIC AREA
LOST? KEEP GOING — YOU ARE MAKING
   GOOD TIME ANYWAY
NEXT TIME TAKE THE COOL ROUTE GO UNDERGROUND
NO FISHING WITHIN 100 YARDS OF THE ROAD
NO FISHING — SUCKERS
NO HUNTING DOGS IN THIS AREA —
   YOU CAN'T FIND ONE ANYWAY
NO TRESSPASSING — THIS AREA IS FOR THE BIRDS
NUDE SWIMMING PROHIBITED IN THIS AREA
NUDIST AREA — KEEP EYES ON ROAD —
   COWBOYS PLEASE REMOVE SPURS
NUDISTS TRY OUR BEAR GREASE FOR THAT SLICK LOOK
OUR GAS CONTAINS LANOLIN — IT KEEPS YOUR
   PISTONS SOFT AND LOVELY
PETRIFIED FOREST — UNIONIZED WOODPECKERS KEEP OUT

**RICK JUST 🦎 SPEAKING OF IDAHO HISTORY SERIES 🦎**

PETRIFIED WATERMELONS — TAKE ONE HOME TO
   YOUR MOTHER-IN-LAW
PRISON AREA — DO NOT PICK UP HITCHIKERS
QUIET PLEASE — ENTERING GHOST TOWN
QUIET PLEASE — HOOT OWLS ARE SLEEPING
RAIN CHECKS CASHED, SUCKERS WELCOME —
   BANK OF SNAKE RIVER
RATTLESHAKE PICNIC GROUNDS — TOURISTS WELCOME
READ TO RESTLESS KIDS (THE RIOT ACT)
REPORT INDIAN MASSACRES TO YOUR DOCTOR
REPORT SMOKE SIGNALS TO WESTERN UNION
   (10 WESTERN COUNTIES)
REPORT SNAKES TO YOUR DOCTOR
RUNNING RABBITS HAVE RIGHT OF WAY
S* BOMB FALLOUT AREA — *SKUNK
SAGE BRUSH IS FREE — TAKE SOME HOME TO YOUR
   MOTHER-IN-LAW
SAVE LIKE MAD — FEARLESS FARRIS — STINKER STATION
SHEEPHERDERS HEADED FOR TOWN HAVE THE
   RIGHT OF WAY
SITE OF DUST BOWL GAME — FARMERS VS GOPHERS
SITE OF POLECAT MASSACRE — IDAHO'S
   GREATEST POLITICAL STINK
SITTING BULL STOOD UP HERE
SKUNK CROSSING AHEAD — CLOSE WINDOWS
SMOKERS PUT OUT YOUR BURNING BUTTS —
   REMEMBER, BUFFALO CHIPS ARE FLAMMABLE
SOUND BARRIER BROKEN HERE — WATCH OUT
   FOR PIECES
STATE HIGHWAY OBSTACLE COURSE
THE EYES OF TAXES ARE UPON YOU
THE ONLY CORN RAISED IN THE DESERT ARE THESE SIGNS
THINK BIG — RAISE ELEPHANTS
THIS AREA IS FOR THE BIRDS — IT'S FOWL TERRITORY
THIS IS NOT SAGE BRUSH! YOU'RE IN IDAHO CLOVER
THIS IS SHEEP COUNTRY —
   LET US PULL THE WOOL OVER YOUR EYES
THIS ROAD FOR WOMEN ONLY — MEN TAKE DETOUR —
   UNLESS ACCOMPANIED BY WIFE OR GUARDIAN

## SYMBOLS, SIGNS, & SONGS

UNLAWFUL TO SPEAR SALMON OR SHOOT CRAPS IN THIS AREA
WANT A COOL MILLION? TAKE HOME A FROZEN ANTHILL
WARNING TO TOURISTS — DO NOT LAUGH AT THE NATIVES
WARNING — BOISE IS FULL OF TAXPAYERS
WARNING — DO NOT DISTURB BREEDING REACTORS
  (SKUNKS)
WARNING — DO NOT FEED OR DISTURB NESTING COYOTES
WARNING — LIONS, MOOSE, ELK, EAGLES PAY YOUR DUES
WARNING — METHODISTS WATCH OUT FOR
  MORMON CRICKETS
WARNING — THE WIND WILL BLOW THIS ROAD
WATCH FOR SNOWSLIDES AND SUNDOGS
WEEKEND DRIVERS, USE OUR PRICKLY PEAR CUSHIONS —
  GIVES YOU A LIFT
WELCOME TO POTOMAC — SLOW DOWN — THIS IS A
  ONE HEARSE TOWN
WELCOME TO UGLY MEN AND BEAUTIFUL WOMEN
WHAT'S EATING YOU? THE NATIVES ARE NOT CANNIBALS
WHY BE A WAGE SLAVE? FIND YOUR WIFE A JOB
WHY BE DISAGREEABLE? WITH A LITTLE EFFORT
  YOU CAN BE A STINKER
WHY GO TO SIBERIA? WORK IN OUR SALT MINES
WITH A LATER START YOU WOULDN'T BE HERE YET
WRITE TO YOUR PEN PALS — THE PAROLE BOARD

# GHOSTLY LAKE HAZEL

Lake Hazel Road runs from Maple Grove Road in Boise to South Robinson Road in Nampa. I have received requests from some who wonder where the heck the lake was?

The answer is, there is no Lake Hazel, but there was once. Sort of.

Back in the early 1900s, there was a move to create reservoirs to capture Boise River water for irrigation. Potential water users contracted with David R. Hubbard, a local landowner, to excavate reservoirs called Painter Lake, Hubbard Lake (later Hubbard Reservoir), Kuna Lake, Watkins Lake, Catherine Lake, and Rawson Lake. These were to be connected by lateral canals. All except Rawson Lake were completed. In the meantime, the much larger Boise Project came along with the promise to bring irrigation to the valley. The lakes were abandoned because they would likely interfere with the Boise Project. Since they were not being used for water storage, all the lakes disappeared in later years, except for Hubbard Reservoir.

So, what does all this have to do with Lake Hazel? Painter Lake was renamed Lake Hazel at some point. Even with the new name, it was fated to be a lake in name only with no water in evidence.

Thanks to Madeline Kelley Buckendorf, who did the research in 2003 for a National Register of Historic Places application.

# MUFFLER MEN AREN'T ALL MEN

You'd think a 25-foot-tall man born in 1967 would have enough documentation behind him to have his story told accurately, wouldn't you?

Not so with the lumberjack that stands at 1405 Main Avenue in St. Maries. You'll see stories about him that say he's standing in front of the High School, where the sports teams are called the Lumberjacks. Well, the high school isn't far away, but he's really on the lawn of an elementary school. And, is he standing? He's not sitting, but he also doesn't have feet, so…

*There are four "Muffler Men" in Idaho. Note that one of them is a woman and none of them sell mufflers. Big Don cleans up at the Museum of Clean in Pocatello. Courtesy of the Museum of Clean.*

Often, you'll see the lumberjack referred to as Paul Bunyan. He's really a generic lumberjack. He's also a Muffler Man.

What? It turns out that giant fiberglass men are referred to in general as Muffler Men. The St. Maries man is holding an axe, but many of the early giants held mufflers in their hands to advertise automotive service shops. The vast majority of them were made in California by International Fiberglass, a boat builder, beginning in 1962. The first Muffler Man was actually a lumberjack. Specifically, it was a Paul Bunyan statue used to advertise a restaurant in Arizona on Route 66.

Thousands of them were made over the years from the same mold, but with some variations. They were cheap—$1,000 to $3,000—and caught one's attention. They held all kinds of jobs, promoting gas stations, restaurants, and roadside attractions. They were dressed as Vikings, football players, astronauts, pirates, soldiers, chefs, and cowboys. There's a cowboy along the interstate near Wendell holding a stop sign in his hands, hoping you'll stop by an RV dealership.

The third known Muffler Man in Idaho has a cushy job. He doesn't even have to stand outside in the weather. Big Don, as he's known, towers inside Pocatello's Museum of Clean, where he wields a giant mop. Needless to say, he's spotless. Word is that he has a cowboy hat too, but he doesn't wear it indoors.

Although the lumberjack in St. Maries is generically a Muffler Man, he's specifically a Texaco "Big Friendly." There were originally some 500 of them, but only a half dozen exist today. He's a little taller than the average Muffler Man, although there's the issue of the feet. There's a story that says he arrived with his feet on backwards so those were chopped off and he was mounted in concrete. There's also a rumor that the lumberjack fell off a truck or was found in the woods.

Wherever the St. Maries' lumberjack came from, he's not the only one of his kind in Idaho. His brothers in Wendell and Pocatello also have at least one sister in the state, a Jackie Kennedy Onassis lookalike in Blackfoot. Her name is Martha, and she advertises Martha's Café. She was *born* a Uniroyal gal. There are maybe a dozen of them left around the country. Martha is conservatively dressed, but she originally hit the streets wearing a bikini.

# JUST WHAT ARE THEY PROTESTING?

**P**rotest Road in Boise has always intrigued me. What protest was it commemorating? Women's suffrage, perhaps? Something to do with a labor strike from back in the Wobbly days? Maybe it came from the civil rights struggle.

As it turns out, Protest Road is named such because of a protest. Over a road. That road.

In March 1950, stakes were going up in South Boise for a new road that would connect the area to a new fire station being built on the rim above. That wasn't a surprise. Residents had voted to construct such a road. But in the mind of a citizen protest committee, the stakes indicated the road was being planned in the wrong place. The road as staked out would send fire engines to Boise Avenue, where they would have to reverse their direction and come back into South Boise along a narrow and twisting thoroughfare. Some residents thought they had voted on a route that would allow engines to access South Boise more directly.

More than 500 citizens showed up to the early community meetings on the matter. They voted to form the South Boise Citizens Protest Committee. Ultimately, a sensible alignment of the road was proposed that seemed to work for everyone. It was decided that the road should be called Protest Road in commemoration of the efforts of the committee.

This wasn't the first time a citizen protest committee from South Boise had been formed. In an article from 1907, the *Idaho Statesman* headlined, "Citizens of South Boise to Hold an Indignation Meeting Next Tuesday Night." That "indignation" was also over a transportation issue. Specifically, it was over poor rail service to the area.

It's not surprising that residents take their transportation issues seriously in South Boise. Transportation was there before there was a South Boise. The Oregon Trail runs through that section of town.

Thanks to Barbara Perry Bauer for her help with research and for her delightful little book *South Boise Scrapbook*.

# ROCK WRITING

The figures left on stone by aboriginal people in Idaho have long been called rock writing, but it is the wrong name for it. The writing is mostly found along the Snake River. They are a form of communication, but to call them writing is a stretch. These long-lasting messages—which for the purposes of this book I am calling "signs"—are either petroglyphs, which are cut or chipped into the rock surface, or pictographs, which are paintings formed by use of minerals and vegetable dyes mixed with water and grease. The people who produced them had nothing like a standard alphabet or standard symbols. Therefore, *reading* petroglyphs and pictographs is largely a matter of conjecture. One can identify representations of deer, coyotes, or warriors which probably means the artist saw those things. Reading more into it is dicey.

Map Rock, which is near Melba, may be trying to tell us more than the average petroglyph. It seems to be abstract, perhaps representing rivers and trails, ergo a map. Many have tried to interpret it.

Some of the best examples of petroglyphs are easily accessible at Celebration Park which was established as Idaho's only archaeological park in 1989. A walk through the huge basalt melon-gravel deposited by the Bonneville flood reveals petroglyphs one hundred to 10 thousand years old.

*Robert W. Limbert poses on his motorcycle, a 1919 Excelsior, in front of Map Rock, circa 1921. Boise State University Library, Special Collections and Archives.*

# THE ADELMANN BUILDING

**B**uilt in 1902 by Civil War veteran Richard Adelmann, this Boise building was originally only one story. When the second story was added isn't clear. The photo was taken in 1980 when Fong's Tea Garden dominated the structure.

The Adelmann Building still has the corner turret, but the Chinese lettering is long gone. The Stearn's Motor Car Company sign on the southeast side of the building looks like a ghost sign (an old advertising sign on the side of a building that has been preserved). It's not. It was painted in 2000 just to spiff up the blank wall and to pay homage to the repair shop that Richard Adelmann once ran.

*Boise's Adelmann building was constructed in 1902 by Richard Adelmann. In 1980, it was Fong's Tea Garden. Photo by John Margolies. Stearn's Motor Car Company mural on the Adelmann, 2000, by the Letterheads, a national sign-painting organization. Photo by Rick Just.*

# THE SAMPSON ROADS

**H**ave you ever found yourself saying, "Somebody should do something about that"? Charlie Sampson, who often went by C.B., had one of those moments back in 1914. Rather than just letting the thought drift out of his head as you and I would likely do, Sampson took on a little job himself. He began marking highways in Idaho so people wouldn't get lost.

Starting in 1906, Sampson ran the Sampson Music Company in Boise. His specialty was pianos. One of the ads for his pianos was a testimonial that read in part, "I play third grade music already, and my daddy only bought me my piano a little over a year ago."

One day, while making a delivery in the desert south of town, Charlie got lost. That annoyed him. He thought there should be signs along the roads so travelers could find their way. He took that suggestion to local officials. They ignored him. To their surprise, Sampson proved that he was not one to let a good idea die. He began to mark the roads around Boise himself.

Sampson carried a bucket of orange paint with him wherever he went, and painted signs on rocks, trees, barns, bridges, fences... just about anything that didn't move. The routes he marked became known locally as the Sampson Trails. Of course, many of the larger signs also included a few words about the Sampson Music Company. Oh, and you could stop by the store and pick up a free map. By the way, could we interest you in a piano?

It wasn't uncommon in the early days of automobile roads in the U.S. for car clubs to take on the job of marking routes and adding mileage signs to various locations. Since state governments didn't take on the responsibility at that time, the clubs were free to mark roads and install signs of their own invention. Things got confusing when two or more car clubs competed to be the markers of a road, since there wasn't always agreement on which was the main road and which was just a muddy side road. Different colored markings denoted the work of different clubs.

## SYMBOLS, SIGNS, & SONGS

Nothing was standardized. It was a mess. For instance, the first stop sign didn't pop up until 1915 in Detroit, according to an article by Ethen Trex in the December 2010 edition of *Mental Floss*. It was a simple white, square sign with black lettering that was more of a suggestion than a regulation.

Sampson got the jump on car clubs in Idaho, and he did such a good job that he *owned* the Sampson Trails. He even hired a three-man crew to keep the signs in shape, spending thousands of dollars on the project.

In the mid-1920s, the Bureau of Highways decided to put a stop to Sampson's signing. They would sometimes mark a parallel route and paint over Sampson's markers. The highway men, pun intended, claimed Sampson defaced the landscape with his orange paint. He probably did, but the Idaho Legislature didn't buy that argument. They passed a resolution commending Sampson for his efforts and gave him the right to continue marking the Sampson Trails.

Sampson eventually extended his work to five states, marking an astonishing seven thousand miles of road. Early highway maps often used the Sampson identifiers rather than state road names.

Charlie Sampson died in 1935, leaving the task of guiding people along the roadways to others. One who perpetuated Sampson's effort is Cort Conley. His book, *Idaho for the Curious*, was where I first learned about the Sampson Trails. It is probably the best guide available for travelers interested in Idaho history.

*The dot on the rock indicated by the sign in this picture doesn't look like much, but those orange splashes of paint along with a complimentary highway map from Sampson Music of Boise were the best way to know where you were in the early days of driving in Idaho. The photo, courtesy of the Idaho Transportation Department, depicts a 1916 Model T Ford probably somewhere in the Treasure Valley.*

# THE "WORLD FAMOUS" RANCH CLUB

The rearing palomino sign that welcomes visitors to the Ranch Club has had a few owners over the years. The Garden City fixture was established in the mid-1940s when Helen Guyer operated the club, but the Ranch Club didn't start out in Garden City. It was moved there in 1959 when Garden City was a brand-new village. The reason the club moved from its previous location, just outside of New Plymouth, was the same reason Garden City was born: gambling.

In October 1949, John Corlett wrote for the *Idaho Statesman* that, "Slot machines are building new streets, a new park and new buildings in Garden City." The village had been incorporated just five months earlier to take advantage of the fact that Boise had banned slot machines.

Originally only eight blocks long, Garden City was one of Idaho's "Foot-wide towns," so designated by a 1951 article in *Life* magazine. The nickname was coined because 17, mostly rural, areas across the state had incorporated often stretching boundaries along a length of highway to include far-flung residents and to take advantage of Idaho's gambling and liquor laws at the time. Island Park, which still boasts that it has the nation's longest main street, was one of the more famous foot-wides.

Garden City fathers publicly dismissed the idea that they were incorporating only to provide licenses for liquor and gambling establishments. That they applied to Ada County for incorporation just three weeks after Boiseans rejected gambling was only a coincidence.

## SYMBOLS, SIGNS, & SONGS

When the Ranch Club was in New Plymouth, owner Helen Guyer tussled with Payette County over liquor license issues for her establishment. She sold the building to Paul Teters, a former Gonzaga University football star, and he moved it in three sections to Garden City. It was billed as "Boise Valley's finest supper club."

An even dozen gambling clubs popped up in Garden City, attracting Boiseans by the hundreds. The Statesman reported that, "The clubs are filled to capacity nightly and there is a lineup in front of each slot machine."

The civic windfall for Garden City included 45 percent of the take from each machine; that lasted only a few years. Idaho outlawed gambling in 1954. By that time, Garden City had gained a reputation for condoning just about anything when it came to zoning, so it was still an attractive option for those who wanted to do business with Boiseans but didn't want a lot of red tape.

Today, Garden City has largely shrugged off its nefarious beginnings. It's the home of the Western Idaho Fair, Plantation Golf Course, and the site of several desirable housing developments. Its zoning laws are fairly typical for a well-run city of its size.

The Ranch Club is one of the few physical reminders of the city's roots. It became just another bar and restaurant in 1954 when gambling went away. The club got a boost in 1980 when that rearing palomino had a brief appearance in the Clint Eastwood movie, *Bronco Billy*. That may have been when the "World's Famous" sign was added to the front of the building. Worldwide fame may be a stretch, but that horse ranks right up there with the Vista Avenue washerwoman and the Capri's giant rooster as valley icons.

# SOMETHING'S FISHY HERE

Unique is a word that needs no modifier since it means "unlike anything else." One thing can't be more unique than another thing. That doesn't stop people from sticking words such as "totally," "really," "completely," and "very" in front of unique. Nowadays its meaning is all but synonymous with "unusual." Language changes and words get watered down. Insert sigh here.

This minor rant cropped up because the word "unique" fit the Fish Inn better than any other word. If there was another building remotely like this one, I'm unaware of it. It looked like a fish, more or less. You entered through the gaping mouth. The body of the fish was covered with shingles made to look like scales. The tail, as the only flat part of the fish, became a sign.

The restaurant was built in 1932 for Kenny and Mamie West on Highway 10 near Wolf Lodge Bay. The look of the thing would lead one to believe that they served fish there. They did. Not exclusively, though. For instance, they served adult beverages. In later years you could have a burger and listen to the Normal Fishing Tackle Band. It was once voted one of the best road bars in America by *Road and Track* magazine.

You could also tack a dollar bill to the ceiling. That not-unique tradition started when a customer proposed to his girlfriend on a dollar bill. She is said to have written "yes," also on a dollar. There were something like four thousand dollar bills tacked to the ceiling at one time. Unfortunately, no one had taken them to the bank when the bills, and the restaurant, burned in 1996.

Fish Inn on old Route 10, was a Coeur d'Alene icon for many years. Constructed in 1932, it served as a local bar and restaurant until it burned in 1996. The photo was taken in 1987 by John Margolies.

# GONE TO THE DOGS

If you're a dog lover, you know how it goes. First, one shows up on your back step looking a little mangy and lost. You adopt her. Then a friend needs to rehome that St. Bernard because they're moving into an apartment. Then puppies happen.

That's not exactly how Dennis Sullivan and Francis Conklin became the dog people of Cottonwood, but the dogs did grow in number and in size until they ended up with one you could sleep in.

Talk about a service dog. This one has a bed—with 26 dogs carved into the headboard—a library, games, and a deck. Bonus: Breakfast!

Sweet Willie, as the bed-and-breakfast dog is called, harkens back to the days when entrepreneurs would entice people off early highways with buildings shaped to resemble something else: coffee pot gas stations, shoe houses, and restaurants shaped like milk bottles.

Building a dog that you could spend the night in wasn't the original idea. Dennis Sullivan was a self-taught chainsaw artist. He buzzed out all kinds of critters, including moose, bear, and cats. His specialty was dogs. Every breed imaginable. His big break came in 1995 when QVC television started selling his work.

That provided the means to open a little store in Cottonwood next to Idaho's only north-south highway, US 95. When demand for his dog art started to be more than he could handle, his wife, Francis Conklin, picked up a chainsaw and learned to carve canines.

Their store, called Dog Bark Park, is easily spotted next to the highway. They thought they'd take advantage of that. The result was a 12-foot-tall beagle named Toby. That brought people in off the highway. So, if a really big dog attracted traffic, what about a really, really big dog? That's when Sweet Willy took shape.

That unique bowser got them a little publicity. This book isn't big enough to list all the places they've been featured. Sweet Willy, AKA the Dog Bark Park Inn, has been featured on the *Ellen DeGeneres Show*, *The Today Show*, in *Ripley's Believe it or Not*, *O Magazine*, *Reader's Digest Best of America*, and on Frommers.com.

In recent years, Francis and Dennis have built a traveling dog called Roamer. He's a beagle that sits on the back of a pickup with his nose in the wind and his paws on the roof. Look for him in a parade near you.

Photo by John Margolies.

# YOU SAY POTATO

Earlier in this book I mentioned that I was not enamored with advertising Idaho potatoes on my car. Though I shun those Famous Potatoes plates, I do like the product itself, and I admire the often-odd advertising the Idaho Potato Commission comes up with.

Big potatoes on trucks were featured on postcards for decades. In 2012, the Commission decided to bring those giant spuds closer to reality by, well, putting a big potato on a truck. The 72-foot-long truck carries a four-ton imitation potato all over the United States. It was supposed to be a one-year promotion in celebration of the 75th Anniversary of the Idaho Potato Commission. It proved so popular that they've kept the big spud rolling.

The truck can be booked for fund-raisers and other events where a giant potato is a must. At the time this was written, the Tater Team consisted of three young women, Melissa the driver, and Kaylee and Jessica the "Tater Twins," whose job it was to talk up taters.

Touring for seven years took its toll on the original potato. So, in 2019 former Tater Team member, Kristi Wolf, decided to turn the tuber that was being replaced by a new spud into an Airbnb rental. The chance to sleep in a 24-foot-long potato has attracted attention from the *Today Show*, *Buzzfeed*, *People*, *Fox News* and many other media outlets.

# SONGS

# A REVOLUTION IN ROCK

Paul Dick was born in Boise in 1942. He worked as a barber in his teens, then he later purchased a Boise drive-in restaurant. In the early 60s, a delivery boy named Mark Lindsay showed up at that drive-in. He was delivering bread, but that wasn't his real mission. Lindsay was a singer and he wanted to be part of a rock and roll band the owner of the drive-in led. Mr. Dick told Mark he could join the band if he learned to play an instrument. Lindsay went home to Cambridge, Idaho and promptly learned how to play the saxophone. It wasn't long before Paul Revere Dick decided to become Paul Revere. Meanwhile, Mark Lindsay, Mike Smith, Phil Volk, and Jim Valley became the original Raiders.

Paul Revere and the Raiders cut their first record in the spring of 1963 at a small Portland recording studio. The record got some airplay, but for some reason the song "Louie, Louie" didn't catch on. A Seattle group, the Kingsmen, later recorded it and turned the song into a rock classic.

Despite that false start, Paul Revere and the Raiders were not just another garage band. They went on to have monster hits of their own, including "Kicks," "Indian Reservation," and "Hungry." They became the house-band for Dick Clark's network television show, *Where the Action Is*.

Revere, who along with his bandmates, dressed in Revolutionary-War-ish costumes, was known as the "Madman of Rock and Roll." During their concerts Revere would chatter on between (and often during) songs with a running comedy routine that included props, puppets, and puns. The Raiders were always moving, mostly jumping up and down to the music. It may not have been choreography, strictly. Or dancing.

## SYMBOLS, SIGNS, & SONGS

The band had some big hits. "Kicks" and "Good Thing" each made it to number four on the *Billboard* Hot 100. "Indian Reservation," which sold nearly four million records, made it to number one, and was their only Platinum Record. Paul Revere passed away in 2014. He was still living in Idaho at the time.

*In this 1967 publicity photo of Paul Revere and the Raiders, we have from the left, Paul Revere, Mike "Smitty" Smith, Phil "Fang" Volk, Mark Lindsay, and Drake Levin. That's Dick Clark pretending to be a drummer. The band evolved from what was originally a Caldwell High School dance band. When Revere took it over, the name of the band became the Downbeats before changing it to Paul Revere and the Raiders. Some of the band members came and went, but Paul was always Paul. He often played his keyboard behind the front end of a car chopped down to the right size, retaining its wheels and tires. Until doing exhaustive research on the subject, I thought he always used the front end of a 1966 Mustang. That's the one on display in the Idaho State Museum. He also performed with a 1965 Mustang façade hiding his org... keyboard. But wait! There's more! He also used a 1957 Nash Metropolitan as a stage prop. Easily his ugliest keyboard-concealer was a 1958 Edsel, or an unfortunate wad of fiberglass shaped to look like one. To add verisimilitude, the headlights and turn signals flashed when the band got really wound up.*

# THE SONG OF THE WEST

If any song deserves inclusion in a chapter about Idaho songs, it is the song of coyotes. So says the author.

If you raise sheep, it's almost a foregone conclusion that you aren't a fan of coyotes. Arguments rage over just how many sheep are killed by coyotes each year in Idaho, but the predators enjoy an occasional lamb chop.

Coyotes aren't picky eaters. They consume mostly small rodents and rabbits, but they seldom turn up their nose at any meal, animal or vegetable. They would love to eat what your dog eats. Maybe your dog, if Fluffy is small enough.

Coyotes are a lot like dogs. They're intelligent. They bark like dogs, and they look a lot like Bowser and Ol' Blue. Although, a coyote's nose is pointier than most dogs, and his tail is bushier, they are related closely enough to cross breed with domestic dogs.

When they run—at speeds up to 40 miles per hour—coyotes hold their tail down between their hind legs. They share that unique trait with only one other dog-like creature, the red wolf. Coyotes are typically shy, nocturnal creatures. You're more likely to hear them than see them. They seem to love singing to the moon. What would a Western movie be without the sound of coyotes? If you hear one of those moon songs, you can try singing back to a coyote. They will often answer your call.

Native Americans greatly admired coyotes. A common character in their stories, Coyote sometimes plays the part of a man, sometimes an animal, and sometimes a god. The creation story of the Nez Perce involves Coyote tricking a monster into swallowing him. Coyote frees all the animals the monster had swallowed and cuts up its parts to form many tribes, saving the heart of the monster for the creation of the Nez Perce.

You can see the Heart of the Monster near Kamiah, Idaho, where the National Park Service retells that Coyote story. If you're lucky, you might hear the trickster's song.

# A FLIGHT ON THE TENUOUS CONNECTION REDEYE

Okay, rock-and-rollers, we're going on a little journey, so buckle in. This will take an airplane to get from where we're starting to where we're going. Maybe a starship.

Marcus and Narcissa Whitman, along with Henry Harmon Spalding and Elizabeth Hart Spalding, were Presbyterian missionaries and were the first people to roll into what is now Idaho. Literally, they had the first set of wheels to enter the country. Four wheels were on a wagon that got them almost to Fort Hall in 1836 before they decided that a cart would work better to cross the desert. So, they took two wheels off and converted the wagon to a cart.

The Spaldings set up the first mission in Lapwai, not far from what would become Lewiston. The Whitman's mission was near Walla Walla. They were killed by Indians, and we don't have time to tell that whole story, so off we fly.

From our perch in the metaphorical sky we spot Perrin Beza Whitman, the adopted son and nephew, of Marcus and Narcissa. He survived the massacre because he was in the Dalles, Oregon Territory, on an errand when it happened. Zooming across the years to 1863, Perrin Whitman is seen moving to Lapwai to work as an interpreter in the Indian schools. In 1883, he and his family moved to Lewiston where he became a trusted businessman for his remaining years, passing away in 1899.

Here's where we swoop to pick up the trail of Perrin Whitman's daughter, Elizabeth Auzella "Lizzie" Whitman, born in 1856. We're picking up speed, so skipping to 1875 we find Lizzie marrying Harry K. Barnett, a title company executive in Lewiston. Lizzie was a singer, entertaining the community with her voice and playing guitar and violin. No time for a standing ovation though, because we're back in the air and following Lizzie's son, Marcus—no doubt named after the murdered Marcus.

Marcus Barton had a wife, but we're going too fast to mention her—nearing light speed now. Marcus had a daughter who was named Virginia. Virginia—buckle in tight—met a man named Wilford Wing at the University of Washington where both were students.
They married and had some kids, one of whom they named Grace Barnett Wing, born in 1939. The family ended up in Palo Alto, California, where Grace went to high school before building the nearby city of San Francisco out of rock-and-roll.

And that's the Marcus and Narcissa Whitman—and Idaho—connection to Grace Slick, one of rock-and-roll's greats and the lead singer of Jefferson Airplane-cum-Jefferson Starship.

*Idaho has some strong connections to popular music. Grace Slick has a tenuous, though interesting, connection. You may not even roll your eyes.*

# MISS IDAHO MAKES GOOD

**J**udy Lynn was a country star you didn't hear much on the radio. Born Judy Lynn Voiten in Boise in 1936, she was just a teenager when she joined a touring company of the Grand Ole Opry. At 19, she was crowned Miss Idaho.

Lynn put out 14 albums and 47 singles. Only four of the singles cracked the country charts, with 1962's "Footsteps of a Fool" doing the best, peaking at number seven.

But radio wasn't Judy Lynn's venue. Vegas was. She had her own show on The Strip for more than 20 years.

*Miss Idaho of 1955 would become Judy Lynn, a country music artist (cowgirl publicity photo) who performed on the Vegas strip for over 20 years. The Miss Idaho photo is courtesy of the Idaho State Historical Society, P2006-20-00438.*

# THAT HOT. ROD. LINCOLN.

Charlie Ryan played one night at the Paradise Club in Lewiston. On his way home to Spokane, he raced his '41 Lincoln against a friend in a Caddy up the Lewiston grade. It was a seat-grabbing race that etched into the memory of the singer. Later he would write lyrics, moving the fictional race to California on a road called Grapevine. Why? Artistic license, I suppose. Grapevine has the necessary two syllables for the line, while Lewiston would have been an awkward three. But another reason is probably that Grapevine is a straight shot, not like the spiral highway in Lewiston. The song doesn't mention a corner at the end of every line, so that long highway worked better. It was called Grapevine not because it was twisty, but because they had to slash through a lot of grapevines when building the road.

Charlie's song was something of a response to a 1951 song called "Hot Rod Race," by Arkie Shelby. There was a series of four back-and-forth racing songs.

Ryan released "Hot Rod Lincoln" in 1955 and did pretty well with it. The 45 stayed on the *Billboard* chart for about a month. Charlie was on the charts again with the same song in 1959. Johnny Bond picked it up in 1960. His version was on the *Billboard* chart for seven weeks and climbed as high as 26. Then in 1971, Commander Cody and His Lost Planet Airmen released what would be the most popular version of the song, reaching number 9 on the charts. On a side note, George Frayne IV, alias Commander Cody, was born July 19, 1944 in Boise, Idaho. Over the years the song was certified to have sold more than a million records.

Commander Cody and crew may have had the big hit, but they did something that ruffled the feathers of many hot rod purists. They changed the Lincoln's V-12 to a V-8. Shocking!

And, was there a real Hot Rod Lincoln? As mentioned above, yes. But Charlie built a second, nicer version of the car to match the song and toured with it as an attention grabber. The candy apple red 1934 Model A with the Lincoln V-12 sold in 2013 for $97,000 to an Ohio doctor who used it as a charity fundraising prop.

One mystery remains about the song, though, at least for me. Here's the line:

"That Model A VitImix makes it look like a pup."

What is VitImix? At the risk of sounding like Google, did he mean Vitamix, which is a brand of blender? Some reader in the know will set me straight.

Charlie Ryan, who is in the Rockabilly Hall of Fame, died in 2008 at 92.

# IDAHO IN LYRICS

According to the website lyrics.com, there are 245 songs that include a reference to Idaho in their lyrics. These range from Frank Black's "Demon Girl" to Dinah Shore's "Dear Hearts and Gentle People." There are many versions of the same song among those 254 mentions, so don't let it go to your panhandle, Idaho.

Giving you sample lyrics from some of those songs would be a public service, but— and I hate to use technical jargon here—music publishers are notoriously hinky about song lyrics appearing in print. Getting permission to print a song snippet is a continuous game of email tag usually ending in the writer simply giving up and becoming something useful like an auto mechanic.

One song I grew up listening to was Vaughn Monroe's rendition of "Idaho State Fair." Perhaps it is a stretch to say I grew up listening to it. I heard it every year for a couple of weeks in September in advertisements for the Idaho State Fair, which is in Blackfoot. The lyrics, which I cannot replicate here for fear of having my fingernails removed by licensing goons, go something like, "(popular pronoun for referring to oneself) found (popular pronoun for referring to someone of the female gender) and (the opposite of found) (popular pronoun for referring to someone of the female gender) at the (name of your favorite state) state fair." It is rather catchy, don't you think?

Perhaps the song with Idaho in the lyrics that immediately pops to mind is "Private Idaho," the 1991 hit by the B-52s. There are some rich and thoughtful lyrics in that song, but you remember it as "I'm living in my own (song title)" repeated about eleventeen times. That's so unfair. Go look up the lyrics yourself so my fingers can keep their keratin.

Those living in Idaho who even now are trying to drive the chorus of "Private Idaho" from their head may be surprised to learn the song only got up to 74 on the *Billboard* Hot 100. It reached number 11 in Australia, where they probably didn't understand the lyrics.

## SYMBOLS, SIGNS, & SONGS

Well, really, who did? And what was it about? Fred Schneider, who wrote the song, said the title was a play on Private Eye. He'd never been to Idaho, and he didn't know much about it except that it was beautiful and was the home to right-wing politics.

Careful as we have to be about including song lyrics in a book, we need not worry about titles. Titles can't be copyrighted. That was good news for Gus Van Sant who appropriated the B-52s song for the title of his 1991 movie, *My Own Private Idaho*, which was about an hour and 45 minutes long. I swear I had to go cut the grass three times while watching it. Okay, maybe it was based loosely on Shakespeare's *Henry IV, Part 1*, *Henry IV, Part 2*, and *Henry V*, but I may have missed the allusions while bagging grass.

That copyright rule is also good news for an Idaho author named Rick Just, whose 1995 book, *Keeping Private Idaho*, is about xenophobia. As it turned out, Idahoans had more interest in practicing it than reading about it.

# KING OF THE ROAD

There seems to be one indisputable fact about Roger Miller's hit, "King of the Road." He wrote it. But where did he write it? That this would even be a question of interest is somewhat puzzling. Sure, it was a big hit. But why would people argue about its provenance?

Miller's concert chat seems to have been the reason for the confusion. He would often toss out a line about where he wrote the song, or where he first saw the sign that became the first line about trailers being sold or rented. He mentioned seeing it in Chicago, Kitchener, Ontario, and Indiana. He bought a little statue of a hobo some place he said inspired him. One of those places where he claimed to have purchased the little hobo was the Boise airport.

Miller often said from the stage that he wrote the song in Boise, Idaho. I like that version because I heard it first from a man who claimed to have been there when it was written.

*Roger Miller told countless stories about how his song, "King of the Road," came about. There's good evidence that it was written, at least in part, during one of his appearances at the Snake River Stampede while he was staying at the Hotel Boise.*

## SYMBOLS, SIGNS, & SONGS

Bob Weisenberger was the manager of KGEM radio in Boise, where I worked for about six years. It was the leading country music station in the valley. Weisenberger said that he was sitting in a hotel room listening to Roger Miller jam with Boxcar Willie, following Miller's performance at Nampa's Snake River Stampede. Boxcar Willie became a concert draw himself over the following couple of decades, especially in Europe, and he even had a minor hit with a cover of "King of the Road." He became a Grand Ole Opry member and was one of the first country artists to open a theater in Branson, Missouri. At the time this story took place, probably 1964, Boxcar Willie was a disc jockey at KGEM, using the name Marty Martin.

Many reports about the genesis of "King of the Road" say it was written at the Idanha. It's such an iconic Boise hotel that those reports just seem right. Maybe not. Miller reminded the crowd gathered for a Stampede promotional press conference in 1972 that he had written the song while staying at the Hotel Boise which is now the Hoff Building. Weisenberger also recalled that it was at the Hotel Boise.

Wherever he wrote it — it was probably written over a period of at least weeks, perhaps coming together finally in Boise—Miller would never need to push a broom for two hours for his accommodations after its release. The song won 1965 Grammy awards for Best Contemporary Rock 'N Roll Single, Best Contemporary Vocal Performance, Best Country & Western Recording, Best Country Vocal Performance, and Best Country Song.

And to think it all started in Boise. Probably.

# IDAHO'S CHAMPAGNE LADY

There is that famous "Peanuts" bit where Lucy talks Charlie Brown into kicking the football, then pulls it away as he falls on his back booting the air. I'm reminded about poor Charlie Brown when I think of Norma Zimmer.

Zimmer was the Champagne Lady on the Lawrence Welk Show for 22 years. She's in this book because she was born in Larson, Idaho which is east of Mullan nearly on the Montana line.

The lady with Idaho roots had been a radio vocalist for years and sang backup vocals for Frank Sinatra, Perry Como, Dean Martin, and Bing Crosby. Her voice is on Crosby's classic "White Christmas."

Norma Zimmer got her job as the new Champagne Lady after Lawrence Welk fired the original singer, Alice Lon, in 1959 for showing too much leg. Norma became the official Champagne Lady on New Year's Eve 1960.

After touring with Welk for three years, Zimmer decided to quit show business and raise her family. Welk said she could quit touring, but he still wanted her on the TV show to sing one or two songs and often dance with him through the bubbles. She still wanted to quit completely, so Welk made her a proposition about those TV appearances. He'd bring a new singer on and "audition" her during the show. Zimmer could leave once he found an appropriate replacement. She reminds me of Charlie Brown because the singers came on to "audition" every week, week after week, for something like 19 years.

According to *Variety*, Norma Zimmer appeared on one episode of *I Love Lucy*, in one film with Bing Crosby, and sang the part of the White Rose in Disney's *Alice in Wonderland*.

Norma Zimmer passed away at 87 in 2011.

*Norma Zimmer, longtime "Champagne Lady" for Lawrence Welk, was born in Idaho.*

# THE BOISE SONGS

There is, perhaps, no quicker way to set a long-time Boise resident's teeth to grinding than to call the town "Boy-zee." If you don't pronounce it "Boy-see," slap yourself in the face with this book right now.

Even so, audiences usually overlook the faux pas when the star on stage panders out to the audience, "Hello, Boy-zee!" Unless, of course, they happen to be on stage in Pocatello at the time.

In the summer of 2010, Jewel played at Outlaw Field in Boise and endeared herself to the audience, despite a couple of false starts, by singing a newly penned title, "The Boise Song." The lyrics list letters you can find in the names of certain cities, i.e., an A in Atlanta, a Y in Kansas City, etc., but ending each verse with "But there is no Z in Boise."

You can easily find it with Google, but if you missed that concert, you might never hear her perform it live, unless she comes back to Idaho. According to Setlist.com, which covers concert statistics, Jewel has performed it just that one time in public.

If you search for Boise in the lyrics of songs, you'll come up with about 50 occurrences. Many are versions of the same song brought out on different albums. Most are obscure.

"What's Your Name" by Lynyrd Skynyrd made a big splash with the opening line, "It's 8 o'clock in Boy-zee, Idaho," released in 1977. According to Songfacts.com the original line to that song was "It's 8 o'clock and boys it's time to go." Ronnie Van Zant's brother, Don Van Zant was opening the national tour of his band .38 Special in Boise. Ronnie, who wrote the song, changed the line to fit the venue. Three days after they released the album, three members of Lynyrd Skynyrd, including Ronnie Van Zant, were killed in a plane crash. "What's Your Name," peaked on the Billboard chart at number 13 in March 1978, probably making it the most popular song containing a reference to the state. It appeared on nine Lynyrd Skynyrd albums.

## SYMBOLS, SIGNS, & SONGS

Boise popped up in the lyrics to a Harry Chapin song, "WOLD." Those were the call letters of the Boise radio station where the singer/DJ had hit rock bottom. As a former Boise DJ, I probably resent the implication. Chapin ignored the fact that all radio station call letters west of the Mississippi begin with a K. In the east, you'll find W call letters, except for KDKA in Pittsburgh. But I digress. The song made it to number 34 on *Billboard's* Hot One Hundred.

Drake (featuring Lil Wayne and Andre 3000) obliquely mentioned Boise in the 2011 song "The Real Her." It was a little hat-tip to the Blue Turf. The word was a little on the fence Z/S-wise, but it would probably make a native smile.

# SOME MORE TENUOUS CONNECTIONS

**G**ary Puckett, lead singer of Gary Puckett and the Union Gap, graduated from Twin Falls High School in 1960. For a couple of years in the late sixties, the group blasted from AM radio antennae all over the country with hits like "Lady Willpower," "Woman, Woman," and "Over You." Their biggest seller was "Young Girl," which made it to number two on the *Billboard* Hot 100. They got edged out for Best New Artist in the 1969 Grammy Awards by Jose Feliciano.

Glenn Close, who has Emmys, Tonys, Golden Globes, and several Academy Award nominations probably doesn't consider her performance as the lead singer of Up with People during the 1965 World Boy Scout Jamboree at Farragut State Park the high point of her career. Still, there you have it.

Lana Turner, who was born Julia Jean Turner in Wallace, Idaho in 1921 was a Hollywood icon. All those apocryphal Hollywood "discovered in a soda shop" stories lead back to her. She was spotted at the Top Hat Malt Shop on Sunset Boulevard sipping Coke while skipping a typing class at Hollywood High. The publisher of *Hollywood Reporter* did the spotting. She was not a singer, but staying with the rules of this book (which I make up as I go along), she is included here because of the reference to the star from Idaho in the song "My Baby Just Cares for Me," by Nina Simone, Natalie Cole, and others.

Bonus tenuous connection: Singer Lana Del Ray took the Lana part of her stage name from Lana Turner. Director Mervyn LeRoy assigned the name Lana to Turner, who legally changed her name to match her film persona.

*Lana Turner wasn't a singer. She's included here because the Idaho native's stage name became part of the lyrics of "My Baby Just Cares for Me." This is a publicity photo from the 1966 film* Madame X *in which she starred.*

# A SONG WITH A HISTORY

"Garden of Paradise" was the title Sallie Hume Douglas gave to her composition copyrighted in 1915. Over the years, at least four people have taken credit for writing lyrics to that music. With various combinations of verse and chorus, "Garden of Paradise" was called "Our Idaho," "Old Idaho," and finally "Here We Have Idaho," our state song. It's a song that has grown and changed and even went through a period of what you might call juvenile delinquency.

Before it became the state song, "Here We Have Idaho" was the school song of the University of Idaho. They called it "Our Idaho" or "Old Idaho." At that time, there was some question over which was the official version and who wrote the lyrics. No one knew who wrote the music. No one, that is, except the composer who discovered her song was being used without permission. She threatened to sue the University of Idaho, and in 1930, they reluctantly purchased rights to the song. In 1931, "Here We Have Idaho" became the state song.

Over the years, there were many arguments over adaptations of the lyrics. The composer of the music threatened another lawsuit. And Idahoans just went on singing of Idaho.

# "THE HOUSE THE CARPENTERS BUILT"

You've probably heard a song written by Boisean Steve Eaton and didn't even know it. He's written songs recorded by Ann Murray, Lee Greenwood, Glen Campbell, the Righteous Brothers, Art Garfunkel, the Fifth Dimension, and others. He once called his then home in Pocatello, "the house The Carpenters built." Kind of a double entendre, that. He wasn't referring to the folks who handled the hammers. It was his hit song, "All You Get from Love is a Love Song," sung by brother and sister Richard and Karen Carpenter, the pop duo of the 70s and 80s, that built the house.

Eaton formed a band called King Charles and The Counts in Pocatello. He and the band members dropped out of high school and moved to Hollywood. They got a record contract with a small label, Charger Crusader Records. Then in the early 70s he formed the band Fat Chance, which signed with RCA. They performed at The Troubadour in Los Angeles and opened for British pop band Yes on a national tour.

Fat Chance didn't last long. When they broke up, Eaton got a contract with Capitol Records for a couple of albums. Recently YouTube program, "How Was that Not a Hit?" highlighted one of Eaton's early records, "Hey Mr. Dreamer." It was episode eight.

Today royalties keep rolling in for his songwriting, and he performs two or three nights a week around Boise. He continues to write and has received a couple of Emmy nominations for music written for PBS specials.

*Songwriter and singer Steve Eaton often performs around Boise. He has passed his talent for entertaining onto his sons, singer/songwriter Marcus Eaton who has several albums under his belt and A.J. Eaton who directed the documentary* David Crosby: Remember My Name.

# THE ABSOLUTELY INDISPUTABLE ORIGIN OF THE HOKEY POKEY

"You put your right foot…," and that's about all you need to get your mind humming the "Hokey Pokey" if you've heard it even once. The rest of the song is a simultaneous instruction manual for how to do the dance.

You would think the origins of such a song would be fairly easy to trace, and you'd be right. The trouble is, there are multiple origins.

According to a 2018 article written for *Mental Floss* by Eddie Deezen, there were similar songs popping up all over the world, nearly at the same time. That would be called "going viral" today, but this was back in the 1940s. Were all the similar songs original, or had the catchy tune earwormed into the composer's heads and come out later as their own creations?

There was much haggling among those who had written songs called "The Hoey Oka" (1940) and "The Hokey Cokey" (1942), both published in the United Kingdom. Another composer was entertaining the troops with his "Hokey Pokey" in wartime London.

Those British songs were news to two composers in Scranton, Pennsylvania in 1946 when they came out with their dance tune called, "The Hokey Pokey Dance."

Though similar, none of those songs was quite the one you've likely heard. That one came out of Sun Valley, which is why we're rattling on about a song that you've never pulled up on Spotify (note: you could).

Charles Mack, Taft Baker, and Larry Laprise, known as The Sun Valley Trio, played "The Hokey Pokey" for skiers at Sun Valley in 1949. The Scranton composers sued, but Laprise won the court case and the right to claim "The Hokey Pokey" as his.

**RICK JUST 🏃 SPEAKING OF IDAHO HISTORY SERIES 🏃**

In 1953, Ray Anthony's Orchestra recorded and released the version you are likely familiar with. It went to number 13 on the charts. The flip side was also a hit, called "The Bunny Hop."

So, there's a solid Idaho connection to "The Hokey Pokey," but don't start moving those celebrating feet yet. There's more to the story. Even those early 40s versions were about 114 years after the fact. A similar dance with similar instructions was published in 1826 in Robert Chambers' *Popular Rhymes of Scotland*. Speculation is that the traditional folk dance had been around since the 1700s. The song, or something like it, showed up in 1857 in the United States when a couple of sisters from England were visiting New Hampshire and passed along the steps to locals there. You know the steps. "You put your right foot…"

# THE GOVERNOR DID NOT LIKE THAT SONG

**R**osalie Sorrels was a much beloved Idaho folksinger and storyteller. Not universally beloved, however. Governor Don Samuelson was one who didn't care for her or her lyrics.

Folk music has a long, proud history of political involvement, and Rosalie never shied away from a cause she believed in. In 1970, the cause was saving the White Clouds from a proposed open pit molybdenum mine at the base of Castle Peak. The song, "White Clouds," was not intentionally an eye poke for Governor Samuelson, though he took it that way. It was a poetic appeal to save wilderness from commercial encroachment and pollution. It wasn't so much that Rosalie's song annoyed the governor as it riled him that a state employee sang it.

Stacy Gebhards was the Idaho Department of Fish and Game's fishery management supervisor in 1970. Gebhards performed "White Clouds" at several events rallying support to save the mountain from development.

*Rosalie Sorrels photo courtesy of Shelley Ross.*

He and two of his friends also performed it at a state dinner at which Interior Secretary Walter G. Hickel was in attendance. Governor Samuelson was there too, and when the accompanying slide show displayed dramatic shots of pollution around the state, Samuelson began steaming. Hickel later gave Gebhards a personal commendation and congratulatory letter, but word came from the governor's office that if he ever sang the song in public again, Gebhards would be fired.

Paul Swenson, a writer for the *Deseret News* out of Salt Lake quoted an unnamed source saying, "The governor blew his stack."

Gebhards kept his job. Rosalie Sorrels kept writing and singing. Samuelson lost the next election to Cecil D. Andrus, and Castle Peak remains pristine today. Rosalie passed away in 2017.

Much of the information for this piece came from Rosalie Sorrels' book, *Way Out in Idaho: A Celebration of Songs and Stories*.

www.ingramcontent.com/pod-product-compliance
Lightning Source LLC
Chambersburg PA
CBHW070437010526
44118CB00014B/2076